Great Game to 9/11

A Concise History of Afghanistan's International Relations

Michael R. Rouland

AIR
FORCE
History
and
Museums
PROGRAM

Washington, D.C.
2014

Engaging the World

The ENGAGING THE WORLD series focuses on U.S. involvement around the globe, primarily in the post-Cold War period. It includes peacekeeping and humanitarian missions as well as Operation Enduring Freedom and Operation Iraqi Freedom—all missions in which the U.S. Air Force has been integrally involved. It will also document developments within the Air Force and the Department of Defense.

Great Game to 9/11

GREAT GAME TO 9/11 was initially begun as an introduction for a larger work on U.S./coalition involvement in Afghanistan. It provides essential information for an understanding of how this isolated country has, over centuries, become a battleground for world powers. Although an overview, this study draws on primary-source material to present a detailed examination of U.S.-Afghan relations prior to Operation Enduring Freedom.

Contents

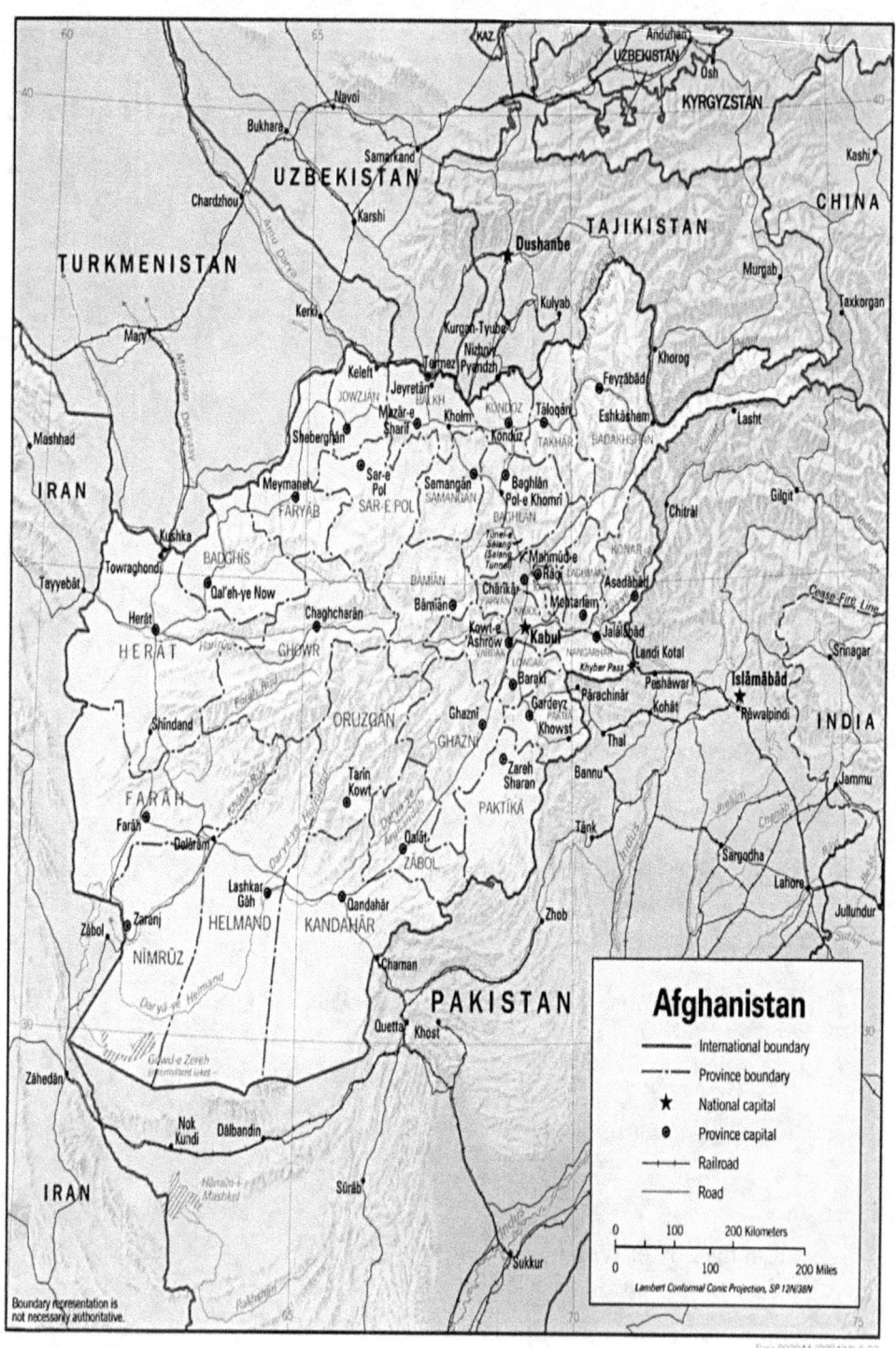

The Razor's Edge

In 1907, Lord George Nathaniel Curzon observed from his time in South Asia the precarious balance on the borderlands of Afghanistan and its impact on the world: "Frontiers are indeed the razor's edge on which hang suspended the modern issues of war and peace, of life and death to nations."[1] From the British-Russian "Great Game" rivalry that started in the nineteenth century to Operation Enduring Freedom in the twenty-first, Afghanistan, despite its remote location and often dysfunctional government, has continued to claim the attention of the world's great powers.

In addition to the Europeans, for almost a century, U.S. leaders have considered economic and strategic interests and the careful balance of power in the South Asia region. These concerns returned to public view in the first decade of the twenty-first century, but the experiences of the past reveal patterns in Afghanistan of weak political regimes, tribal unrest, and diplomatic intrigue.

A review of modern Afghan history raises two important questions: how did ethnic politics shape Afghanistan's national policy, and how did Soviet and U.S. strategic interests influence Afghanistan's international affairs? To answer these questions, a narrow focus on Afghan history after the 1979 Soviet invasion or on U.S. links to the mujahideen is of limited utility. A broader, albeit concise, examination of the long-term structures of Afghan domestic politics and international diplomacy offers a fuller understanding of this complex region.

Afghanistan's path from empire to nation-state in the eighteenth and nineteenth centuries established enduring conditions for ethnic conflict and resistance to modernization in the twentieth and twenty-first centuries. Its turbulent history has been marked by recurring patterns of political centralization, then concessions to tribal authorities; resistance to foreign influence, then foreign intervention; and support for modernization, then reaction against it. These tensions have plagued Afghanistan throughout its history.

Long before the Cold War standoff between the United States and the Soviet Union and the subsequent conflicts between al-Qaeda and the West, Afghanistan endured centuries as a frontier zone between larger opposing empires: Persian in Western Asia; Mughal in South Asia; and Turkic in Central Asia. Economically, the area has remained on the margins. Even when Peshawar, Ghazni, Turquoise Mountain (Ghor), and Kandahar emerged as metropoles during the indigenous Kushan (first to third centuries), Ghaznavid (tenth to twelfth centuries), Ghorid (twelfth to thirteenth centuries), or Durrani (eighteenth to nineteenth centuries) Empires, their income was drawn from their Persian or Indian dominions.

Afghanistan was constrained by mountainous barriers that created particular ethnic and tribal allegiances. The foundation of the early Afghan state rested on confederations of core groups that projected power outward rather than establishing strong, centralized political rule from within. From the mid-tenth century to the mid-eighteenth century, the rulers of Afghanistan were of Turco-Mongolian origin or led a military dominated by Turco-Mongolians. Not until the Durrani Empire did ethnic Pashtuns emerge as a political force in Afghanistan.[2] Thus it is crucial to consider Pashtun rule in the context of Afghanistan's rich multiethnic heritage.[3] In *Afghanistan's Endless War*, Larry P. Goodson observed: "If Afghanistan has been marked by a history of invasion and conquest, no less has it suffered from almost continuous internal strife among the native peoples living in its remote mountain valleys."[4]

Complicating matters, the Pashtun ethnic group itself has historically been fractured and subjected to shifting alliances. Pashtun rivalries, particularly between the Durrani and Ghilzai tribes, remain an important feature of a multifaceted ethnic battlefield. While the rivalries subsided after the rule of Abdur Rahman Khan (r. 1880–1901), the socialist experiment after 1978 reignited them. Ghilzais and eastern Pashtuns played leading roles in the People's Democratic Party of Afghanistan (PDPA, Hizb-e-Demokratik-e-Khalq-e-Afghanistan), in several mujahideen groups, and in the Taliban. Durranis returned to power with Hamid Karzai at the end of 2001.

In addition to the Pashtuns and their ongoing competition for power, other ethnic groups have used their leverage and geographic advantages to play key roles in Afghan history. In particular, Tajiks, Hazaras, Uzbeks, Aimaks, Turkmen, Balochs, Nuristani, and Kuchi have made contributions to the viability of the Afghan state. Their involvement in military, economic, and political enterprises in Afghanistan has been important, and so has their drive to establish an enduring Afghan nation-state, despite deeply rooted ethnic ties and trade across its borders. Rather than continued existence as a buffer zone created by imperious neighbors—Russian, Persian, British,

2

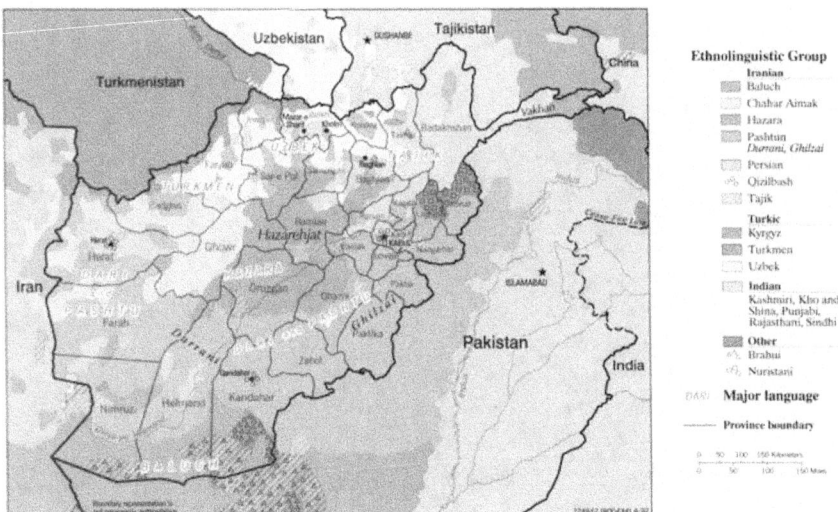

A Central Intelligence Agency map of ethnolinguistic groups in Afghanistan as of 1992, based on data collected by the U.S. Bureau of Census. *Library of Congress.*

and later Pakistani—Afghanistan emerged as a confederation of tribes with a developing national identity.

Returning to the realities on the ground, mapping and understanding the intricacies of ethnic ties in Afghanistan remain difficult. Intermarriage, bilingualism, and shared local identity (*manteqa*), to mention but a few factors, have consistently undermined the idea of solidarity along ethnic lines.[5] The modern Afghan state reveals the complexities of its role as ruler and as subject of successive frontier empires.

3

ONE

Origins of the Afghan State, the Great Game, and Afghan Nationalism

In the early eighteenth century, the territory that came to be known as Afghanistan was divided between the Safavid (Persian) and Mughal (Turco-Mongol) Empires. Ahmad Shah commanded a military unit under the ascendant Persian ruler Nadir Shah in his campaigns against the Mughals. When Nadir Shah was assassinated in 1747 and the Safavid Empire collapsed, Ahmad Shah (r. 1747–72/73) established an independent city-state around Kandahar. He adopted the name "Dur-i-Durran," or "Prince of Pearls," and used the term "Durrani" to distinguish the tribes affiliated with him. According to an early-nineteenth-century British account, Afghanistan after Ahmad Shah became an "orgy of intrigue, treachery, torture and murder . . . [an] ever-shifting kaleidoscope of betrayal."[1] Ahmad Shah Durrani and his son Timur Shah Durrani (r. 1772/73–93) expanded their domain, conquering territories from Kashmir to the Arabian Sea and from the Amu River (da Amu Sind) to the Indus River (Abasin). The Durrani realm at the end of the eighteenth century included modern-day Afghanistan and most of Pakistan, making it the second-largest Muslim empire of its day.

Ahmad Shah Durrani, poet, warrior, and king that he was, wrote of his nostalgia for Afghanistan during ten campaigns to expand his rule over Kashmir, Punjab, and Sind:

> Whatever countries I conquer in the world,
> I would never forget your beautiful gardens.
> When I remember the summits of your beautiful mountains
> I forget the greatness of the Delhi throne.[2]

This fondness for his Afghan homeland provided a lasting challenge to his heirs. Unlike the rulers of other Central Asian empires who moved their capitals to strategic and economically viable locations, Ahmad Shah consolidated power in the Pashtun bases of Kandahar, Kabul, and Peshawar. Thus the Durrani Empire was "a coat worn inside out," according to Thomas J. Barfield.[3] Kandahar, Kabul, and Peshawar were poor and sparsely populated compared to the rest of the Durrani Empire. The wealthiest territories remained on frontiers in every direction.

British penetration into South Asia in the eighteenth century created another layer of challenges for future Afghan leaders. Afghans unintentionally aided British occupation of the Pashtun borderlands and, more critically, allowed the rise of Sikh power in Punjab.[4] Once Durrani's descendants destroyed the Mughal Empire, they could not maintain such a vast and diverse empire and prolong their dominance over Kabul, Kandahar, Herat, the Hindu Kush, Peshawar, Punjab, Kashmir, Baluchistan, and Sind. Moreover, each time the Durrani leader left his seat of power in Kandahar, emerging plots from rival Pashtun tribes and other ethnic groups threatened to depose him.[5] Afghan rulers slowly lost their territories to the Sikhs and the British: Punjab (1801), Kashmir (1819), Sind (1820s), Peshawar (1834/1879), and Baluchistan (1879), until Abdur Rahman Khan focused his authority in Kabul, Kandahar, Herat, and the northern Afghan provinces in the 1880s. As of this writing, four urban centers remain: Kandahar in the south, Herat in the west, Balkh in the north, and Kabul in the east. Peshawar and the North-West Frontier Province (now Khyber-Pakhtunkhwa) make a fifth region, which the British gave to Pakistan in 1947. Peshawar was historically important to Afghan rulers as their summer capital and continues to be strategically significant as the eastern gateway to the Khyber Pass, the link between Central and South Asia.[6]

Hoping to counter both internal and external threats, Afghan ruler Dost Mohammad Khan (r. 1826–39, 1842–63) attempted to ally himself with the British as early as the 1820s and curtailed relations with Persia and Russia. However, the inability of the British to agree on the return of Peshawar to Afghanistan impeded Anglo-Afghan cooperation. Sikhs maintained de facto rule over Peshawar after 1818, and while British forces could not quell Pashtun violence on the northwestern frontier, they preferred a Sikh alliance with an emphasis on Punjab territories. Ultimately, Dost Mohammad could not accept the permanent loss of Peshawar and British intransigence, and he turned to the Russians for help in 1838.[7] At the same time, British government agent Alexander Burnes had been negotiating to restrain the maharaja of the Sikh Empire, Ranjit Singh, from taking more territory as an inducement to convince Dost Mohammad not to join a Russo-Persian alliance. The British, however, did not provide adequate assurances to protect Afghanistan against Russia. A Russian military mission took advantage of Dost Mohammad's failure to gain concessions from the British and offered to defend Afghan territory against Ranjit Singh.

"SAVE ME FROM MY FRIENDS!"

"IF AT THIS MOMENT IT HAS BEEN DECIDED TO INVADE THE AMEER'S TERRITORY, WE ARE ACTING IN PURSUANCE OF A POLICY WHICH IN ITS INTENTION HAS BEEN UNIFORMLY *FRIENDLY* TO AFGHANISTAN."—*Times*, Nov. 21.

This *Punch* political cartoon from November 30, 1878, shows the "Great Game" at its fullest, with the Afghan amir caught between the Russian bear and the British lion.

The negotiations were not completed by the time British forces invaded Afghanistan to secure geopolitical interests in South Asia, resulting in the First Anglo-Afghan War (1839–42). The conflict ended with an inglorious British withdrawal, while Afghanistan abandoned its Russo-Persian ties. This was the first gambit in the Anglo-Russian rivalry—the "Great Game"—that would plague Afghanistan during the nineteenth century.[8]

External pressures from Persia, Russia, and British India forced Afghanistan to focus on consolidating power in the provinces between those empires. Afghan rulers sought to strengthen their own rule while deterring the territorial interests of their neighbors. An example of the latter occurred when Dost Mohammad wrote to Sir John Lawrence, viceroy of India, in 1867, noting, "We have men and we have rocks in plenty, but we have nothing else."[9] In a 2011 study, Joseph J. Collins observed that "in a great political paradox, Afghan rulers were strongest within their nation when they were supported by foreign subsidies."[10] British funding and arms ultimately provided the cornerstone of a defensive bulwark against Russia in Afghanistan.

Dost Mohammad was the first Afghan ruler to consult with foreign military advisors. During Burnes's visits in the 1830s, Dost Mohammad sought his guidance on conscription.[11] Although he failed to recruit Burnes, he invited a menagerie of American, French, English, Persian, and Indian adventurers and military deserters into his retinue. Josiah Harlan, a West Point graduate from Pennsylvania, was one of the first and most prominent Americans known to have maintained residency in Afghanistan. Historian Sir John William Kaye described Harlan in 1851 as "an American adventurer, now a doctor and now a general, who was ready to take any kind of service, with any one disposed to pay him."[12] Having previously served Ranjit Singh, Harlan moved to Afghanistan and quickly became involved in several revolutionary and military intrigues. Ultimately, he became an aide de camp for Dost Mohammad and helped prepare the Afghan infantry for the Battle of Jamrud (1837) and the defense of the Khyber Pass against Ranjit Singh.[13]

After Dost Mohammad, the Afghan leader most associated with military modernization was his grandson, Abdur Rahman Khan (r. 1880–1901). Historian Vartan Gregorian observed that "Abdur Rahman relied heavily on a military autocracy to guarantee his absolutism. Perhaps the 'Iron Amir's' greatest single achievement was the creation of a standing and centralized Afghan army."[14] By the 1880s, Abdur Rahman had a standing army of 50,000 to 60,000 men. He also positioned grain in Herat, Kandahar, and Kabul to support expeditionary missions against recalcitrant tribes. Barnett R. Rubin described his rule as a "coercive-intensive path to state formation."[15] While his campaign aimed to establish a modern state that circumvented tribal rule, Abdur Rahman faced seventeen major rebellions in a fifteen-year period.[16] Expressing a sentiment that would be repeated several times hence, Abdur Rahman cautioned: "I had to put in order all those hundreds of petty chiefs, plunderers, robbers and cut-throats, who were the cause of everlasting trouble in Afghanistan. This necessitated breaking down the feudal and tribal system and substituting one grand community under one law and one rule."[17]

Anthropologist Thomas J. Barfield noted that Abdur Rahman "abolished the decentralized governmental system in which tribes and regions maintained a high degree of autonomy in exchange for submitting to the legal authority of the Kabul government. When faced with numerous revolts by his own relatives and regional groups, he waged war against his own people until he and his government had no rivals of any type."[18] To establish his authority throughout Afghanistan, Abdur Rahman singled out Ghilzai Pashtuns and Hazaras during punitive campaigns in the 1880s and 1890s. He was particularly brutal in reprisals against Hazaras, who sought to guard their autonomy while Abdur Rahman centralized state power and checked the influence of local chiefs. As Abdur Rahman explained, "I am

Abdur Rahman Khan, the "Iron Amir," ruled Afghanistan from 1880 until his death in 1901. During his effort to establish a modern state, his government faced seventeen major rebellions in a fifteen-year period.

quite wearied of the behaviour of these people. They should take with them their families and household property and go out of the country, and I will populate their country with Afghans."[19]

Ghilzai Pashtuns, the traditional rivals of the Durranis, also suffered from forced migrations in the late 1880s and early 1890s. Abdur Rahman moved thousands of Ghilzai from the south and east to north of the Hindu Kush, depriving them of a Pashtun base in the south and creating a pro-Pashtun population amid the Tajiks, Turkmen, Uzbeks, and Hazaras in the central and northern parts of Afghanistan.[20] This action weakened the ability of Ghilzai Pashtuns to coalesce and further diluted the economic and political influence of non-Pashtuns, whose land was often seized.[21] Ultimately, Abdur Rahman established Durrani Pashtuns as the privileged ethnic group in Afghanistan, and a pattern of their over-representation in the government began.[22] These actions would have significant strategic and political implications for the twentieth century.

In the early 1890s, while Afghan identity remained localized and regional, rather than national, Abdur Rahman created a centralized state bureaucracy that placed Afghans into one consistent governmental system of taxation, administration, and military recruitment that drew them into a nascent Afghan state. Abdur Rahman centralized his authority by keeping his sons in Kabul and dispatching loyal followers as provincial governors. He created a supreme council and a general assembly (*loya jirga*) with representatives from the royal family (*sardars*), local elites from around the nation (*khawanin mulki*), and religious leaders (mullahs).[23] He also created new provinces that undermined traditional ethnic and tribal boundaries.

Abdur Rahman did not offer much in exchange for the divestiture of power from the regions and the supremacy of the elite in Kabul, however. He did not invest in infrastructure, education, communication systems, or transport networks. "Afghanistan's level of urbanization was higher in the fifteenth century under the Timurids, when Herat and Balkh were international centers of culture and commerce," Barfield noted, "something that late-nineteenth century Kabul (with a population of only fifty thousand) never came close to achieving."[24]

Returning to the international arena and following his defeat in the Second Anglo-Afghan War (1878–80), with the subsequent occupation of his territory by the British, Abdur Rahman became well aware of the new geopolitical realities of the Great Game. In his memoir, he asked the rhetorical question: "How can a small power like Afghanistan, which is like a goat between two lions, or a grain of wheat between these two strong millstones of the grinding mill, stand in the midway of the stones without being crushed to death?"[25] His answer was to develop an isolationist policy and reject commercial ties with his neighbors. "The greatest safety of Afghanistan lies in its natural impregnable position," Abdur Rahman wrote, for "Allah has given us every peak of the mountains for a fortress of nature, and foreigners know that the Afghans, being born warriors, can go on fighting for ever and ever, as long as they can hide themselves behind the stones and do not have to face the enemy in the open field."[26] Abdur Rahman's observation proved to be an enduring one, as Coalition forces in Afghanistan reported the use of these same tactics by Afghan insurgents in the twenty-first century.

Dost Mohammad and Abdur Rahman confronted their limited resources and began to define the Afghan nation as a coherent political unit in the second half of the nineteenth century. Both leaders rearranged military and political structures to meet the challenges of modernity with a mix of isolationism, authoritarianism, militarism, and diplomatic skill. Yet while they initiated reforms to manage the diverse territories that remained in Afghanistan, they institutionalized commercial backwardness, ethnic and regional antagonism, and political compromise, leaving the country ill-prepared for the challenges of the twentieth century.

Mohammad Yaqub Khan (*center*) at Gandamak, a village outside of Jalalabad, during May 1879 negotiations that resulted in the Treaty of Gandamak, the document that outlined what became the Durand Line. To his right is Maj. Pierre Louis Cavagnari, who became British Resident in Kabul and was killed by mutinous Afghan troops in September 1879. Photo by John Burke. *British Library.*

ORIGINS OF THE DURAND LINE

One of the defining events in Abdur Rahman's rule was the concession of the Durand Line, which has persisted as an international boundary by agreement since November 12, 1893.[27] This territorial compromise between Britain and Afghanistan confirmed the Treaty of Gandamak, signed on May 26, 1879, by Mohammad Yaqub Khan, son of Sher Ali Khan and, briefly, amir of Afghanistan. Yaqub Khan ceded autonomy of foreign relations to Britain; consented to a British mission in Kabul and deeper commercial relations; and transferred the Khyber Pass, Kurram Valley, the Pishin Valley, including the Bolan Pass, and Sibi in Balochistan, to British India. He did this in exchange for an annual monetary subsidy.

According to Amin Saikal, Abdur Rahman never accepted the Durand Line "as more than a line delineating the Afghan and British responsibilities in the Pashtun tribal areas. He contended that the line could not constitute a permanent border between Afghanistan and British India."[28] Abdur Rahman expressed serious reservations about the agreement with Sir Henry Mortimer Durand, foreign secretary of British India, and other British officials. In a letter to the viceroy of India, Henry Petty-Fitzmaurice, Abdur Rahman recalled that Pashtuns in the North-West Frontier Province "being

11

brave warriors and staunch Mohamedans, would make a very strong force to fight against any power which might invade India or Afghanistan. I will gradually make them peaceful subjects and good friends of Great Britain." He cautioned, however, that "if you should cut them out of my dominions, they will neither be of any use to you nor to me: you will always be engaged in fighting and troubles with them, and they will always go on plundering."[29]

Although Abdur Rahman was aware of the potential consequences of his concession, he did not have many alternatives.[30] He knew that unrest in the frontier regions would continue to undermine British authority, but he wanted to avoid direct conflict with Britain. The British viewed the Durand Line as an opportunity to secure high passes into India and to curb Afghan interests in Baluchistan. Abdur Rahman, on the other hand, understood that his rise to power and authority within Afghanistan rested on British support and subsidies. Abdur Rahman later argued that the British "had not the sense to understand that taking and keeping under British possession all these barren lands on the borders of Afghanistan was a very unwise step, by which they burdened the exchequer of India with the heavy expense of keeping an army on the spot to maintain peace in these territories."[31] To complicate matters, Abdur Rahman extended the practice used by rulers since Dost Mohammad of criticizing the British in public while allying with them in private, advocating jihad against the British while collecting their subsidies. Abdur Rahman believed, however, that his actions slowed imperial encroachment and provided the necessary stability for reforms in Afghanistan.[32]

Responding to the Durand compromise, Abdur Rahman predicted the sustained significance of Afghan unity: "The first and most important advice that I can give to my successors and people to make Afghanistan into a great kingdom is to impress upon their minds the value of *unity*; unity, and unity alone, can make it into a great power. All the royal family, nobility, and people must have one mind, one interest, and one opinion, to safeguard their homes." Abdur Rahman was indeed concerned that the Durand Line would undermine the consolidation of power he had begun a decade earlier: "In your cutting away from me these frontier tribes who are people of my nationality and my religion, you will injure my prestige in the eyes of my subjects, and will make me weak, and my weakness is injurious for your Government."[33]

Although the notion that Afghanistan would function as a buffer between Russia and Britain would take hold a decade later, Abdur Rahman understood Afghanistan's importance to the stability of the region and its strategic place in Asia. In the end, the Durand Line would have lasting implications for the Pashtun borderlands. As a result of the exodus of

Afghan refugees that began during the Soviet occupation in the 1980s, almost twice as many Pashtuns lived in Pakistan as in Afghanistan by the end of the 1990s.[34]

Two

Stasis and Modernization

After Abdur Rahman Khan, Afghanistan entered into a period of sustained stasis, or civil strife. A conventional interpretation of stasis is the balance of equal and opposing forces that results in a kind of stability. In his descriptions of ancient Greece, Thucydides offered a more apt understanding of the political dissolution and violence that accompanies such a stalemate: "In times of peace, neither side had the excuse or the willingness to call in the two great powers, but when the war was on, alliances were easily obtained by those on both sides who, plotting a new order of things, sought through calling in outsiders both to harm their opponents and to acquire power for themselves." As a shifting war between individuals and parties, Thucydides viewed stasis as a cause of social and political disintegration.[1]

When Abdur Rahman died, his eldest son, Habibullah Khan (r. 1901–19), who had been groomed to rule, was prepared to succeed him. In Barnett R. Rubin's words, the "peaceful succession was an event with no precedent and so far, no sequel."[2] Habibullah was not as imperious as his father. He eased restrictions on the tribal elites, reducing their conscription requirements and allowing them more control over local affairs. Habibullah still understood the value of a well-armed, modern standing army, but he viewed economic development as a subsidiary function of military needs.[3]

Seeking allies in his father's former rivals, Habibullah invited back many Afghan exiles, including Peshawar and Naqshbandi (Sufi) elites. Mahmud Beg Tarzi, an intellectual influenced by the nationalist and modernist "Young Turk" movement, was the most influential to return. He founded Afghanistan's first newspaper, *Siraj al-Akbar Afghaniyah* (The Lamp of the News of Afghanistan), which was pan-Islamist and anti-imperialist in orientation. Tarzi believed that the newspaper was "one of the most essential tools of modern civilization."[4] It became a forum for realistic views of Afghanistan's situation. As historian Vartan Gregorian explained, "Tarzi singled out the disunity of the Afghans and their anarchic concept of freedom and law as other factors that had contributed to the backwardness of the country. The disunity was such, he declared, that it had calamitously set city against city, village against village, street against street, tribe against tribe, brother against brother." Gregorian continued:

> In Tarzi's view, one important result of this disunity was that the majority of Afghans had developed a negative concept of freedom, equating freedom with the absence of restraint or governmental authority. He saw lawlessness as historically regressive and as alien to the spirit and elevated ethics of Islam. True freedom, he wrote, lay in adherence to a positive concept of law, a concept in which law is seen as a cohesive and constructive social force contributing to the development of religion, national genius, and civilization.[5]

Using his position, Tarzi sought to root out the causes of social and political disintegration and to address Afghanistan's backwardness.

Influenced by Tarzi, Habibullah pursued the soft power of Afghan nationalism and international recognition of the Afghan nation. In 1901, soon after his succession, he sent envoys to Great Britain, Russia, France, Germany, Japan, China, the Ottoman Empire, Egypt, Persia, and the United States. He followed Abdur Rahman's model of neutrality, using Afghanistan's natural boundaries to his advantage while impeding Russian and British trade concessions.[6]

During this period of internal stability, Habibullah oversaw the development of schools, the construction of the first hospital and hydroelectric plant, and the appearance of wealth in the cities. This latter development marked the beginning of the great social divide between the cities and the countryside. Habibullah also identified the importance of a well-funded, centrally managed, modernized army. In 1904, he founded the Royal Military College (Madrasse-e Harbi-e Sirajieh) for the Durrani Pashtun elite.[7]

Alongside his military reforms, Habibullah invited foreigners to assist and lead several infrastructure development projects. An American, A. C. Jewett, formerly an engineer with the General Electric Company, moved to Afghanistan in 1911 when he was hired by a British company to build an electric generating plant for Habibullah's summer palace at Jabal Saraj in Parwan Province, north of Kabul. By his niece's account, Jewett "soon discovered what later generations of aid providers did—that it is not easy to help Afghans. Jewett's original two-year tour stretched out to seven years while he struggled with physical difficulties, bureaucratic delays, and cultural obstacles."[8]

16

Habibullah Khan (*left*), Abdur Rahman's eldest son, ruled Afghanistan from 1901 until he was assassinated in 1919. His third son, Amanullah Khan (*right*), consolidated power after his father's death. Amanullah instituted a series of unprecedented reforms, but his reforming zeal was not supported by political acumen, and he was overthrown in 1929. He lived in exile in Italy and Switzerland, dying in 1960.

Habibullah's measured reforms encountered the harsh realities of foreign affairs with the Anglo-Russian Convention of 1907. Alarmed by the rising power of Germany, Russian and British leaders sought to end their conflict in Central Asia and to reaffirm Russia's 1873 vow not to invade Afghanistan. According to the 1907 Convention, the British would "exercise their influence in Afghanistan only in a pacific sense," while the Russians, on their part, declared that they "recognize[d] Afghanistan as outside the sphere of Russian influence."[9] Thus the European powers agreed to consult with each other on all matters pertaining to Afghanistan, and they stipulated that Afghanistan would remain neutral. Afghan leaders were incensed when their input was ignored and they had no place in negotiations between Russia and Britain regarding interests in Afghanistan. The Kabul elite developed a severe distrust of both Russia and Britain and rejected, as a threat to national integrity, their requests to expand trade.[10]

When the Ottoman caliphate called for a global jihad against the British and their allies during World War I, Afghanistan sided with the Young Turks. Many in Afghanistan were driven to arms with a feeling of intense resentment of British imperialism. In 1915, a Turkish-German mission arrived in Kabul to prepare an invasion of India, but Habibullah gave only tentative backing to the plans while practicing a policy of neutrality. Before the Treaty of Versailles was signed, however, Afghanistan had a new ruler.[11]

In February 1919, unknown assailants assassinated Habibullah while he was on a hunting expedition. Habibullah's third son, Amanullah (r. 1919–29), who was then in charge of the army and treasury in Kabul, seized power. He eliminated dissent and gained the loyalty of his chief rival and uncle, Nasrullah Khan, who was supported by the *ulema* (legal scholars) and Pashtuns along the Indian border. When Amanullah declared independence at the beginning of his reign on February 28, 1919, he set in motion events that led to the Third Anglo-Afghan War. This conflict lasted from May 3 to August 8, 1919, and consisted of a series of border skirmishes.[12]

To prevent an escalation of the conflict, the British Royal Air Force bombed targets in Jalalabad and Kabul in an early example of air superiority. Using a Handley Page V/1500 heavy bomber developed during World War I, the British dropped one and a half tons of bombs on Jalalabad in a single day and targeted several military installations, an armaments factory, the royal palace, and Abdur Rahman's tomb in Kabul. Combined with the disarray of the Afghan army and the lack of popular support in Pashtun areas of British India, the British aerial offensive forced Amanullah to make a quick concession for peace.[13]

The war ended with the Treaty of Rawalpindi, signed on August 8, 1919, which guaranteed sovereignty to Afghanistan. The agreement confirmed Amanullah's diplomatic independence and freed Afghanistan from British interference in its foreign affairs for the first time since the 1870s.[14] As the price for this independence, Amanullah agreed to uphold the Durand Line, although he continued to support Pashtun disobedience and revolts in British India.[15] For its part, the British Indian government was well aware of the need for pragmatism with Afghanistan. As Lord Chelmsford, viceroy of India, stated in a report to London in October 1919:

> We have to deal with an Afghan nation, impregnated with the world-spirit of self-determination and national freedom, inordinately self-confident in its new-found emancipation from autocracy and in its supposed escape from all menace from Russia, impatient of any restraint on its absolute independence. To expect the Afghanistan of today willingly to accept a Treaty re-embodying our old control over her foreign policy is a manifest impossibility. If we were to impose it at the point of the sword, to what end? The Treaty would have to be torn to shreds the moment the point of the sword was withdrawn.[16]

Afghanistan initiated official foreign relations with Turkey, Persia (Iran), Germany, France, Italy, and, most significantly, the newly formed Soviet Union, which was the first state to recognize Amanullah's government in March 1919.[17] Vladimir I. Lenin decreed Amanullah the leader of "the only independent Muslim state in the world," believing that Afghanistan held great importance as a potential model for Asia. Leon Trotsky, then people's commissar for military and naval affairs, wrote that "the road to Paris and London lies through the towns of Afghanistan, the Punjab, and Bengal," declaring that imperialism alone preserved the capitalist system. Soviet support for Amanullah in 1919 cemented the relationship through the 1920s. As Afghans endeavored to strengthen their independence, the Soviets consolidated power in Central Asia, and anti-British sentiment rose in the region.[18]

The Soviet-Afghan Treaty of Friendship, signed on September 13, 1920, and ratified on February 28, 1921, was the new Soviet government's first international accord. Both parties agreed to refrain from entering agreements with third parties against the interests of the other. As part of the treaty, the Soviets promised to return territory from the Panjdeh oasis seized in 1885, but ultimately they returned little land. The Soviets also offered limited aid to build a radio station in Kabul and a telegraph line from Kabul to Kandahar and to Serhetabat (Kushka), Turkmenistan.[19]

During the 1920s, Afghanistan and Persia were strategically important to the Soviets as a defensive bulwark against the British and as a potential font of anti-British nationalism along the Indian frontier. The Afghan-Soviet relationship, however, was soon tested by competing interests in Central Asia: the Soviets were actively propagating their revolutionary ideology in the region, while Amanullah sought to build a confederation of Islamic states there. The Basmachi Revolt in Soviet Central Asia became a focal point in this rivalry. The *basmachi*, an Uzbek term for bandits, were armed militias led by *kurbashi*, or local chiefs, and inflamed by widespread famine, political uncertainty, and the nationalization of cotton and food production. They were loosely organized groups that became a popular counterrevolutionary and anti-Soviet movement, based in Bukhara, Khiva, and the Fergana Valley.[20]

By December 1921, basmachi forces numbered 20,000 and identified themselves as mujahideen (holy warriors). The Soviets sent Enver Pasha, a former Young Turk, to quell the revolt, but he joined it instead. Amanullah also decided to support the basmachi and sent his best troops with Gen. Mohammad Nadir Khan, the future king, to fight alongside them in Muslim solidarity. In July 1922, Nadir Khan declared to the Soviets that "if the hostile activity of the Bolsheviks against Bukhara does not cease, the Government of Afghanistan will be forced to annex Bukhara. This is the only way to assist a Muslim state in the center of Asia to stand up against Bolshevik intrigues."[21] Enver Pasha led the capture of Dushanbe as the rebellion peaked in 1922, but he could never unify the movement or generate international support. Ultimately, Amanullah's concern over Soviet expansion in Central Asia was less than his fear of civil war caused by British intrigue and Pashtun tribes in the southern and eastern provinces. Amanullah finally agreed in November 1922 to Soviet demands that he withdraw Afghan troops, and he continued a careful balancing act to appease British, Soviet, and pan-Islamic interests.[22]

While Afghan-Soviet relations deteriorated during the revolt, Fedor Raskolnikov, a Red Navy officer, civil war hero, and architect of the Soviet Republic of Gilan, arrived in Kabul in July 1921 as the first all-Soviet Ambassador to Afghanistan. He supported increasing aid to check British influence and to promote his country's anti-imperialist credentials. An important cornerstone of the Afghan-Soviet relationship in the 1920s was the creation of the Royal Afghan Air Force. After the success of British air power during the Third Anglo-Afghan War, Amanullah sought to build air capabilities for his own national army. The Soviet air force arranged for aircraft and weapons to be sent from Italy and flew the first five aircraft to Kabul in 1924. Later, the Afghan government acquired three Junkers from Germany and two British aircraft. By the end of the 1920s, the Royal Afghan Air Force had twenty-five pilots: three Afghan, four German, and eighteen Russian.[23]

When the Khost Rebellion, initiated by Mangal and Ghilzai Pashtuns resisting Amanullah's domestic reforms, broke out in March 1924, the Soviets sent technicians and pilots to help Amanullah subdue the rebels. The Soviets also donated Polikarpov R–1s, Soviet copies of Airco DH–9As, on the condition that Russians would fly them. "From a psychological point of view," Gregorian argued, "the Amir's use of airplanes piloted by Russians and Germans against the rebels was at the least ill-advised. The intrusion of 'infidels' into an internal feud was not only regarded as a sign of weakness but considered irreligious as well."[24] Despite the political ramifications, the use of foreign planes and pilots against the rebels had a positive effect on the growth of Afghan air power. French journalist Maurice Pernot observed at the time that "at the end of October 1924, Russian pilots crossed the Amu Darya, flew over the mountains through the gap at the Bamyan River, and brought their planes up to Kabul. The impression was considerable. Soon after, twenty-five young Afghans departed to Russia in order to learn the craft of aviation." With profound foresight, Pernot wrote in 1927 that Afghan aviation henceforth would

Darul Aman Palace, "The Abode of Peace" or "Abode of Aman[ullah]," was built on the outskirts of Kabul in the 1920s. It is also known as the King's Palace, as the Afghans built a separate residence for Queen Soraya on a nearby hill (see p. 68). Darul Aman housed the Defense Ministry in the 1970s and 1980s. It was restored after fires in 1969 and 1978 but severely damaged during the civil wars of the 1990s. Proposals have circulated to rehabilitate the structure for use by the Afghan parliament. Photo (2009) by Sgt. Teddy Wade, USA. *Department of Defense.*

depend on Russian matériel and personnel. British sources agreed that the Afghan air force was essentially "a Russian service." By 1928, the Soviets had established an air link with Central Asia and the first flights between Kabul, Kandahar, and Herat.[25]

While the birth of Afghan air power was a small but impressive accomplishment, Amanullah's social reforms proved an important milestone in Afghan history. His efforts to modernize Afghanistan exceeded those of his predecessors, Abdur Rahman and Habibullah. Amanullah embraced European advances in education, improved conditions for women, and supported the press. Beginning in the early 1920s, he introduced new taxes, universal conscription, an expansion of the educational system, and changes to family law, including family affairs and marriage customs, as part of a systematic reconstruction of Afghan society.[26] Amanullah directly challenged local traditions and ways of life, prompting rebellions that began in the southeastern city of Khost in 1924.[27]

After the early uprisings subsided, Amanullah and his wife, Soraya, who was the daughter of Mahmud Tarzi, set out on a grand tour in late 1927 that included visits to India, Egypt, Italy, France, Germany, Britain, the Soviet Union, Turkey, and Iran. Amanullah received honorary degrees from Oxford and Berlin Universities, the Collar of the Annunziata from King Victor Emmanuel of Italy, and the Order of the Golden Spur from Pope Pius XI. As he embarked on his travels, Amanullah launched a campaign to end Afghanistan's isolationism and foreign dependency and to transform its political and economic institutions.[28]

In a series of major initiatives from 1927 to 1929, Amanullah presented a secular constitution based on the Turkish model; attempted to define the relationship between religion and the secular establishment while both groups refused to compromise; created an independent judiciary; invested in schools for girls and teachers from Europe and India; expanded legal rights for women; reorganized the tax and budget systems; established a national bank (Bank-e Milli); and set in motion a campaign against nepotism and corruption. This was the most ambitious improvement program in Afghan history, but it was ill-fated from the start. Amanullah's embrace of modernization met with strong reactions from tribal and religious leaders, the traditional power brokers in Afghanistan. According to cultural historian Senzil Nawid, Amanullah sought to "purge the practice of Islam in Afghanistan of its folk ways, traditional taboos, and superstitions, which he claimed were espoused by ignorant and self-interested clergy."[29] Ultimately, his reforming zeal was not supported by political acumen, and his social programs continued to antagonize the tribal elites, religious leaders, and the army.

An uprising of Shinwari Pashtun tribesmen expanded to widespread revolt in 1928, forcing Amanullah to abdicate in January 1929. At the same time, Ghulam Nabi Charkhi, Afghan ambassador to the Soviet Union, crossed the Amu Darya with Soviet forces and briefly occupied Mazar-i Sharif, where his brother had been governor. He found little support for his faction, however, and the Soviets continued to support Amanullah.[30]

The crisis provided an opportunity for Habibullah Kalakani, derided by Pashtuns as "Bacha Saqao" or "son of the water carrier," to seize power. An ethnic Tajik army deserter and charismatic bandit in the style of Robin Hood, he ruled Afghanistan from January to October 1929. As Shinwaris revolted in the east, Wazir tribes arrived from the southeast, and Habibullah Kalahani's group of Tajiks and Ghilzai Pashtuns moved from the north and occupied Kabul. Amanullah, with his attempt to regain power having failed, fled from Kandahar to India in May. Habibullah Kalakani reversed many of Amanullah's reforms, banning western clothing and closing the schools for girls. He also began preparing for battle against another rival, Nadir Khan.[31]

Barakzai Legacies

The earliest rulers of Afghanistan were Sadozai-Popalzai Pashtuns, including Ahmad Shah Durrani and Timur Shah. This order changed in 1826 when Dost Mohammad of the Barakzai clan emerged as the sovereign of Afghanistan. Traditionally, the Barakzai clan served as viziers, the power behind the Sadozai-Popalzai princes. When Dost Mohammad became ruler, many Afghans viewed him as a usurper to the throne. He used the lesser title of amir, rather than shah, in deference to his forebearers, a tradition maintained until Amanullah declared himself *malik* in 1926.[32]

After Amanullah abdicated, Mohammad Nadir Khan (r. 1929–33) enlisted the support of the British and raised an army to remove Habibullah Kalakani from power. Nadir Khan had been a renowned general and former minister of war, but he had been exiled as the Afghan minister to France because of disagreements with Amanullah and Tarzi over the pace of reforms. To secure his succession, Nadir Khan allied with conservatives and arrived in Kabul at the front of a coalition of Amanullah's relatives. Nadir Khan also benefitted from the military leadership of his brothers, Shah Mahmud Khan and Shah Wali Khan, who returned from exile in France with him. Although Nadir Khan had little personal interest in ruling Afghanistan, he acknowledged both his popularity as well as Amanullah's lost mandate when he took the crown.[33]

In 1929, because the Afghan government was weak and bankrupt and the national army had ceased to exist, Nadir Khan made concessions to appease local unrest. He annulled almost all of Amanullah's reforms, confirmed Habibullah Kalakani's enforcement of Islamic law, and reintroduced gender segregation (*purdah*) and the wearing of the veil (*chadri*). He promulgated a new constitution in 1931 that entrenched religious values.

On the international front, Nadir Khan pursued a policy of neutrality and sought to curb Soviet economic and political influence in Afghanistan. He renegotiated the neutrality pact of 1926 and concluded the Treaty of Mutual Neutrality and Non-Aggression with the Soviet Union in June 1931. One clause declared that each state would prevent activities within its territory that "might cause political or military injury."[34]

With respect to military affairs, Nadir Khan moved away from Amanullah's efforts to centralize control of the armed forces. He returned the recruitment process to tribes and clans, even excepting the entire Paktia region from mandatory military service in recognition of its support in ousting Habibullah Kalakani. Nadir Khan also promoted the inclusion of Hazaras, Mangals, and Mohmands in the army.[35]

In 1933, Nadir Khan founded the Maktab-i-Ihzariah, a military preparatory school for the sons of tribal chiefs. This was a distinct departure from the promotion of Durrani elites by Afghan rulers since Abdur Rahman. Nadir Khan's remarks at the launch of the school underlined the renewed importance of the army to uphold stability in Afghanistan:

> An era marked by discords and civil wars has ruined and weakened our native land, and it is only after a series of coordinated efforts that it will be possible to reestablish its might and prosperity. I hope, with the help of almighty God, that Afghanistan may possess a strong and well-organized army that will constitute a beautiful rose on the head of its friends and a thorn in the eye of its enemies—an army that would assure peace and prosperity in our country.[36]

Nadir Shah and his successor Zahir Shah (r. 1933–73) made a lasting, ultimately devastating deal with religious conservatives to curtail the changes instituted by Amanullah. Low literacy and government withdrawal from social reforms meant that educational advances were limited to Kabul, furthering a divide between urban and rural areas. In small steps, Nadir Shah formed commercial ties with Britain and Russia, introduced financial planning, and improved roads through the Hindu Kush.

Nadir Shah was assassinated in Kabul by Abdul Khaliq, son of a Hazara servant of Ghulam Nabi Charkhi, who avenged the killing of his master by Nadir Shah.[37] With Nadir's death, his three surviving brothers rallied around Nadir's nineteen-year-old son, Zahir Shah, who functioned first as a figurehead while his uncles—Mohammad Hashim Khan as prime minister, Shah Wali Khan as minister of war, and Shah Mahmud Khan as minister of the interior—played major political roles in the 1930s and 1940s. In particular, Hashim Khan led Afghanistan toward neutralism and gradualism in foreign policy and provided the foundation for *bi-tarafi*, literally "without sides," the nonalignment strategy of the 1950s and beyond.[38]

As prime minister, Hashim Khan continued the efforts of Nadir Shah to strengthen the army and the economy with foreign assistance. He looked beyond his Soviet and British imperial neighbors to find additional allies to counter their bipolar influences. To this end, Hashim Khan invited German experts and business interests to build hydroelectric and industrial plants. He also forged ties with Japanese and Italian businesses with little British and Soviet awareness of these activities.[39] He used the fear of Soviet aggression to generate loans from the British and Germans to buy arms and confront tribal revolt. Despite the global economic crisis, Afghan leaders avoided enacting heavy taxes by extracting revenue from foreign gosvernments in the form of loans and foreign assistance from the Soviet Union, Britain, Germany, and Japan in the 1930s and 1940s, and then the Soviet Union and the United States after World War II.[40]

In a theme for the era, and an enduring pattern, Afghan leaders not only balanced disparate and competing foreign interests, they also regulated the popular mistrust of outsiders to encourage foreign assistance. Afghanistan's experiences with British military invasions and political hegemony for the better part of a century caused general distrust of Europeans. At the same time, however, the king and his uncles decided that European modernization strategies could fix Afghanistan's political and economic backwardness.[41] As geologist Ernest Fox

Mohammad Zahir Shah in the early 1930s. He became king in 1933 at age nineteen after the assassination of his father, Mohammad Nadir Shah. Zahir Shah reigned for forty years, then lived in exile in Italy after being deposed in 1973.

explained after his time there in the 1930s: "Afghanistan still dislikes the foreigner. The mountaineer's natural love of independence, their strong militant religious sentiment, and centuries of unpleasant experiences with foreign invaders have bred this feeling. But the present Afghan leaders realize that they can employ to advantage the technical achievements of the West."[42]

Afghanistan embraced a more globalized outlook before World War II, becoming a member of the League of Nations on September 27, 1934. On July 8, 1937, Afghanistan joined Iran, Iraq, and Turkey to sign the "Eastern Pact of Friendship and Nonaggression," also known as the Saadabad Pact, which established the inviolability of mutual frontiers and abstention from interference in each other's internal affairs.[43] In seeking these alliances, Afghan leaders positioned themselves as a political force in the Middle East.[44] They also affirmed their diplomatic independence, which had been constrained for a century by the Great Game. On November 6, 1941, as the growing war became more widespread, the Grand Assembly released this statement:

The Afghan nation has at no time been under any obligation to a foreign government, nor will she ever be. The nation has always been free, and will also in the future maintain its free and independent existence. By the help of God, the people of Afghanistan are unanimously prepared to live a life of honor by defending their rights with all their material and spiritual forces, even to the point of shedding the last drop of blood.[45]

While Afghanistan did not endure the same wartime fate as Iran, which was occupied by Soviet and British troops, it did face rampant inflation, abandoned development projects, and reduced foreign trade, which resulted in major economic upheaval.[46] The experience demonstrated to the young ruling elites the vital necessity of economic reform and modernization. When Hashim Khan resigned as prime minister in May 1946, his brother, Shah Mahmud Khan, embarked on an ambitious new modernization plan that would have long-term implications for Afghanistan.

A new challenge also arose in the diplomatic sphere when Afghanistan could no longer play equal sides against each other. There were many among the Afghan elites with German sympathies, but the Afghan government had recognized the consequences of Iran's friendship with Germany and instead chose to remain neutral during the war.[47] Afghanistan's experience during World War II would soon make the United States a key yet elusive ally.

THREE

Early Relations with the United States

When Amanullah Khan began his foreign policy initiatives in the 1920s, he included an effort to open relations with the United States. The U.S. Department of State, however, delayed the discussion of diplomatic recognition. U.S. officials viewed Afghanistan as part of Great Britain's sphere of interest, and they were skeptical of Afghanistan's acceptance of Soviet aid.[1]

Despite these reservations, relations between the United States and Afghanistan remained cordial. In July 1921, Secretary of State Charles Evans Hughes wrote to President Warren G. Harding, "There is a Mission here from Afghanistan apparently with full powers and desirous of having American participation in the development of that country."[2] Harding met the mission, led by Gen. Wali Khan, on July 26, 1921, at the White House. A few days later, he wrote to Amanullah, "It is my wish that the relations between the United States and Afghanistan may always be of a friendly character, and I shall be happy to cooperate with Your Majesty to this end."[3] Relations, however, never progressed beyond epistolary pleasantries during the Harding administration.

In 1925, the Afghan government submitted a draft "treaty of friendship" to renew the discussion of diplomatic relations with the United States.[4] In response, Wallace S. Murray, chief of the State Department division for near eastern affairs, argued that "Afghanistan for centuries has been a cockpit of Anglo-Russian struggle over the control of the principle gateway to India, the Khyber Pass, and there is no reason to believe that this struggle will cease now that Russia is controlled by the Bolsheviks. No foreign lives in the country can be protected and no foreign interests guaranteed."[5]

Afghanistan's inability to safeguard foreigners and its prohibition of missionaries meant that U.S. visitors were limited to adventure travelers. Two such men, Theodore Roosevelt Jr. and Kermit Roosevelt, sons of Theodore Roosevelt, wrote that "the Afghanistan route was very difficult, and the natives uncertain, to put it mildly. We did not wish to be 'collected' ourselves before we had a chance to collect any animals."[6]

Kermit and Theodore Roosevelt Jr. during their 1925–26 expedition in South Asia. They observed that "the Afghanistan route was very difficult, and the natives uncertain, to put it mildly." *Library of Congress.*

Despite U.S. apprehension, Afghan desire for formal diplomatic relations never waned. Mohammad Zahir Shah framed a letter to President Franklin D. Roosevelt in April 1934 with the opening remarks, "My Dear and Most Honoured Friend: In view of the friendship and goodwill, which, since the extraordinary embassy of Afghanistan of 1921, are established between the two great States of Afghanistan and the United States of America." Zahir Shah informed Roosevelt that his father had died and that he had ascended the throne. He continued, "We are pleased to notify the desire of the Afghan Government to strengthen the political and economic relations, which he had and has still now with the High Government of the United States."[7]

Several factors combined to delay U.S. recognition in the 1920s and early 1930s. In 1934, Acting Secretary of State William Phillips wrote to Roosevelt:

مورخهٔ ٦ ثور ١٣١٣
مطابق ٢٦ اپریل
١٩٣٤،

Mohammad Zahir Shah's April 1934 letter to Franklin D. Roosevelt, in the original Dari. Zahir Shah expressed Afghanistan's desire "to strengthen the policial and economic relations" with the United States. *National Archives.*

Our failure to recognize the Government of Nadir Shah was due largely to the fact that this Government was never formally notified of the abdication of Amanullah and the accession of Nadir Shah; moreover, we have been naturally conservative on the subject of establishing relations with Afghanistan owing to the primitive condition of the country, the lack of capitulatory or other guarantees for the safety of foreigners, and the absence of any important American interests."[8]

Thus informed, Roosevelt offered a polite reply without intending to change the status quo: "I cordially reciprocate the sentiments which you express and, in extending recognition to Your Majesty's Government, take this opportunity of assuring you of my hope that friendly relations will always exist between the United States and Afghanistan."[9]

Roosevelt initiated a deliberate process to establish U.S. relations with Afghanistan that culminated in the "Provisional Agreement regarding Friendship, Diplomatic and Consular Representation between the United States and Afghanistan," which was signed in Paris on March 26, 1936.[10] The slow progress toward recognition reflected the economic isolationism and noninterventionist foreign policy of the United States in the 1930s. But a few U.S. commercial interests began to recognize Afghanistan as a potential market. In one such case, U.S. officials supported the first Afghan military purchases from the United States, beginning in February 1935 when the Caterpillar Tractor Company sold fifty tractors to the Afghan army.[11]

A significant expansion of U.S. involvement in Afghanistan took place when the Afghan government offered oil concessions to a U.S. consortium that included Seaboard Oil Company, Texas Oil Company (later known as Texaco), Case, Pomeroy & Company, and Fisher Brothers. The Afghan government granted this group access to oil deposits throughout Afghanistan, with an option for mineral deposits, on November 20, 1936.[12] The agreement called for additional measures and certain infrastructure investment to be completed within the first year after signature. The oil exploration was not fruitful, however, for a number of reasons. Murray, the State Department's chief of division for near eastern affairs, recounted that despite three years of negotiation, which obtained extensive oil concessions in both Afghanistan and Iran, the Seaboard Oil Company suddenly and unexpectedly withdrew from both agreements.[13] Afghan officials did not understand why the United States gave up so quickly, after only one year, despite growing concerns over the global oil market and increasing security concerns in the late 1930s.[14] Although the venture failed, U.S. officials began to realize the need to formalize relations with Afghanistan. Murray had written in July 1937 that "I do not see how we can avoid much longer establishing a permanent legation at the Afghan capital."[15]

Afghanistan's strategic location during World War II prompted the United States to bolster diplomatic relations. When Louis G. Dreyfus Jr., the U.S. minister to Iran, visited Kabul in June 1941, he noted that "the Afghans have a sincere and deep-rooted desire, in the absence of a friend or neighbor to whom they can turn, to have a disinterested third power friend to assist and advise them, and they have always hoped that the U.S. would be willing to fill such a role." Dreyfus believed that "this is an opportunity which should not be missed of establishing ourselves solidly in a strategic position in Asia."[16] When the United States entered the war, Murray expressed an interest in developing a treaty of friendship to replace the provisional accord of March 1936, but he did not pursue that goal.[17]

The requirements of war did result in the establishment of an American legation in Kabul on June 6, 1942. From 1942 to 1945, the first U.S. envoys to Afghanistan included Cornelius Van H. Engert, Ely L. Palmer, and Dreyfus, all experienced diplomats with extensive backgrounds in the region. They directly confronted pro-German sentiments in the Afghan government that could have destabilized the British Indian frontier during the war.

In July 1942, Engert arrived as the first U.S. minister to Afghanistan. In 1922, Engert, then serving as the second secretary of the American legation in Tehran, Iran, had been the first U.S. diplomatic officer to visit Afghanistan. During his subsequent assignment to Washington, he published a confidential study, *A Report on Afghanistan*, about his travels there.[18] This work remained a key reference for U.S. officials until Engert returned during the war, twenty years later. Upon his arrival in Kabul, he informed Secretary of State Cordell Hull that the king of Afghanistan "had for many years harbored feelings of great sympathy, confidence and admiration for the United States."[19]

On the other side of the globe, President Roosevelt welcomed the first Afghan diplomat accredited to the United States, Abdul Hussein Aziz, in 1943.[20] While U.S. officials considered the strategic implications of Afghanistan's geographic location in Asia, including a secret plan for an alternate Lend-Lease route to the Soviet Union and China through Afghanistan and India, Afghan leaders viewed the United States as a potential counter to British and Soviet interests in Asia. Writing to Hull, Engert clarified in November 1943 that "from the Afghan point of view, the U.S. would be the ideal powerful friend to whom to cling especially as pro-British elements are still afraid to give public expression to their feelings."[21]

U.S. officials soon perceived the complexities of Afghanistan's foreign policy challenges. On one hand, Engert optimistically told Hull that "Afghanistan is ready to exercise a stabilizing influence in Central Asia and on the northwest frontier of India provided only that she can be reasonably certain that she will not be ground between the upper and nether millstones of rival powers struggling for supremacy."[22] On the other, U.S. diplomats were aware of Afghan leaders' fear of a return to the nineteenth-century Great Game as the Soviets emerged as a military power during the war. "It is certain that as [a] result of spectacular Russian military successes, Afghan officials have been trying to improve relations with [the] Soviets and to cultivate closer official and social contacts," Engert observed in February 1943. He added that "there are as yet no indications of [the] future course of Soviet policy toward Afghanistan, but Russia has long been a most uncertain neighbor, and little trust is placed here in Soviet promises and undertakings." [23] In a letter to Hull in April 1943, Engert wrote, "The Afghans are convinced that when the war is over Russia will demand substantial territorial concessions of her neighbors and that neither the U.S. nor Great Britain will be able to stop her." [24]

The Afghans' attitudes toward the Soviet Union proved no less problematic than their relations with Great Britain and British India. Following a meeting with the Afghan minister, Aziz, in Washington in November 1943, Hull recounted the official Afghan position: "The Afghan-Indian frontier presented no problem in so long as the British remained in India, but that the Government of Afghanistan would never permit that the Afghan tribesmen along the present northwest frontier of India should be subject against their will to the control of the Indians." Anticipating challenges that would plague Afghanistan in the future, Aziz concluded, according to Hull, that "if the tribesmen in question should by any chance prefer to remain with the Mussulmans [Muslims] of India, Afghanistan would come to them." [25]

The United States and its allies were able to keep foreign conflict from reaching Afghanistan's borders during World War II, and U.S. officials remained interested in the country's potential strategic value. Engert fought to send aid to Afghanistan during the war, despite its neutral status. He also facilitated the export of karakul wool, Afghanistan's primary export commodity, to the United States. This was an extraordinary feat during the privation of war, and it inspired cordial relations with the Afghans over the next decade. [26]

The U.S. Department of War shared little of the State Department's interest in Afghanistan. Col. Harold R. Maddux, chief of the liaison section, War Department General Staff, argued in June 1944 that "the War Department is unable to foresee any military benefits that will accrue to the United States as a result of increased effectiveness of the Afghan army." [27] Two years earlier, Engert had sent a telegram to Hull requesting the placement of several bomber squadrons in northwest India or northeast Persia (Iran) "to bolster his Afghan allies." Engert argued that "in view of immediate urgency of military situation I venture to make a practical suggestion to raise morale of Afghan Government: Arrival of a few American bomber squadrons even if only for purely temporary duty in North and Northeastern Persia would make profound impression in Afghanistan." [28] In May 1943, Engert and the military attaché to Afghanistan had managed to present a Stearman trainer plane to the Royal Afghan Air Force. [29] The proximity of the China-Burma-India theater provided additional opportunities for military cooperation.

A year later, more substantial military-to-military interaction ensued. On December 29, 1944, a C–47 carrying members of the Afghanistan military mission arrived at Hijli Air Base in northern India to visit Maj.

In December 1944, Maj. Gen. Curtis E. LeMay and XX Bomber Command hosted a visit by senior Afghan officers at Hijli Air Base, India. The delegation included Lt. Gen. Mohammad Daud Khan, the king's cousin, who would become prime minister in the 1953. *U.S. Air Force Historical Research Agency.*

Gen. Curtis E. LeMay and XX Bomber Command as part of a tour of the China-Burma-India theater. The mission toured two B–29s at the base, developing rapport and enjoying a halal meal together.[30] Toward the end of the war, Lt. Gen. Mohammad Daud Khan, the king's cousin and commander of the Kabul Army Corps who would become prime minister in the next decade, requested military training for Afghan officers, envisioning a training mission in Afghanistan run by U.S. rather than Turkish advisors. U.S. government officials refused the request, as they did not view Afghanistan as a military ally because it had maintained its neutrality throughout the war.[31]

Since the Soviet-Afghan Treaty of 1931 was still in force at the end of World War II, Afghans would have abrogated their treaty by pursuing deeper ties with the United States, as that would have constituted a third-party alliance. Yet during a visit in November and December 1948, Abdul Majid Zabuli, minister of national economy, requested U.S.-manufactured weapons to maintain internal security in the face of persistent tribal revolt. Zabuli also articulated Afghanistan's potential aid to President Harry S. Truman's containment policy in two official meetings. According to meeting notes, Zabuli asserted that "properly armed and convinced of U.S.

backing, Afghanistan could manage a delaying action in the passes of the Hindu Kush, which would be a contribution to the success of the armed forces of the West." At a meeting three weeks later, he added that "when war came, Afghanistan would of course be overrun and occupied. But the Russians would be unable to pacify the country. Afghanistan could and would pursue guerrilla tactics for an indefinite period."[32]

The United States continued to deny military aid to Afghanistan through the late 1940s and early 1950s as U.S. interests in South Asia began to focus on newly created Pakistan as an increasingly important ally.[33] U.S. diplomat Leon D. Poullada and some others believed that the United States had an "Afghan blind-spot" where "Afghanistan was always mysteriously overlooked or deliberately ignored."[34] More likely, however, the U.S. foreign policy establishment made pragmatic decisions on U.S.-Afghan relations based on what it considered to be reasonable geopolitical and strategic expectations of the region. At that time, Afghanistan remained on the margins of the Cold War, a situation that would change dramatically a few decades later.

POSTWAR GEOPOLITICS AND THE ORIGINS OF THE PASHTUNISTAN DEBATE

While the United States demonstrated little interest in supplying aid to Afghanistan at the end of World War II, Great Britain was more open to the idea.[35] Under the Lancaster Plan, the British started to provide the Afghans with equipment and training and, by 1947, the Afghan army and air force had become dependent on British training and supplies. The partition of India in that same year, however, quickly altered the political landscape of the region.[36]

Through an act of Parliament in July 1947, Great Britain officially partitioned British India into the two independent "dominions" of India and Pakistan. Afghanistan immediately abrogated its treaties with British India and challenged Pakistani claims to British territory along the northwest frontier.[37] Afghanistan specifically rejected Pakistan's intention to uphold the Durand Line as the new international border. On September 30, 1947, Afghanistan was the only United Nations member to vote against the admission of Pakistan. On July 26, 1949, an Afghan *loya jirga* (national council) denounced all Anglo-Afghan frontier accords and ceased to recognize the Pakistani-Afghan boundary.[38] Thus began a prolonged dispute between Afghanistan and Pakistan over the mounting question of "Pashtunistan," the "land of the Pashtuns" that stretches from the Hindu Kush to the Indus River.

From the British perspective, diplomat Sir William Kerr Fraser-Tytler explained, "The British did not solve the problem of the tribes, and when in August, 1947, they handed over the control of India's North-Western defences to the untried Government of Pakistan, they handed over likewise a fluid, difficult situation, fraught with much danger."[39] When the British held a 1947 referendum for the autonomous tribal agencies, including Malakand, Khaibar, Kurram, North Waziristan, and South Waziristan, they offered two alternatives: annexation to India or to Pakistan. The British did not include Afghanistan as a choice since they were aware that the tribal areas of the northwest frontier had entered into international limbo in August 1947. In legal terms, the tribal areas were part of British India rather than India and thus did not become part of either India or Pakistan at independence. British officials determined that "Pakistan would not have been able to raise any legal objection if the tribes had placed themselves under the protection of Afghanistan or if, with the consent of the tribes, the tribal areas had been annexed by Afghanistan."[40] In the end, the inhabitants of the North-West Frontier Province overwhelmingly chose to remain with Pakistan, although many boycotted the referendum.[41]

Afghanistan disputed Pakistan's claims to the frontier provinces, but Pakistan effectively excluded Afghanistan from frontier discussions and responded with a series of partial blockades in 1948 that would last intermittently for more than a decade.[42] In the most severe cases, open conflict arose, as in March 1949 when the Pakistani air force bombed Moghulgay in Khost Province as part of a territorial dispute. For its part, the Royal Afghan Air Force dropped anti-Pakistani leaflets in border areas. In addition, Afghan tribal forces staged unofficial cross-border raids in 1950 and 1951 that were supported by the Afghan National Army. These efforts had little impact other than to antagonize the Pakistani government. On the domestic front, Mohammad Daud Khan, as minister for tribal affairs, in November 1949 established the Khushal Khan Khattak School for Pakistani Pashtuns to study in Kabul.[43] During this formative period, Daud became the leading advocate for Pashtunistan, and his policies as prime minister (1953–63) and president (1973–78) were a major obstacle to normalizing relations with Pakistan.

Despite the efforts of Afghan politicians, the United States did not take an active role in the Pashtunistan dispute. Prince Mohammad Naim, after he left his post as chargé d'affaires in Washington in July 1949, announced that he was "deeply disappointed" because he found U.S. policy on Pashtunistan and toward Afghanistan in general "one of complete disinterest and indifference," according to State Department cables.[44] On the contrary, U.S. policy makers were deeply concerned with the strategic implications of the territorial conflagration. Louis Dreyfus, U.S. ambassador in Kabul from 1949 to 1951, feared that the dispute could push Afghans toward the Soviets. The official policy as of February 1951 read:

> Our interests would be seriously prejudiced by the failure of Afghanistan and Pakistan to reach an accord on matters of tribal status and treatment. . . . We should continue to encourage Afghanistan to settle its differences with Pakistan and to promote the regional cooperation which will preclude its excessive commercial dependence upon the USSR which has obvious implications for Afghan independence.[45]

Out of public view, U.S. officials tried to broker a deal as they developed Pakistan into a strategic ally, but Pakistan would not commit. Meanwhile, the Afghan government pursued two public and concurrent diplomatic maneuvers. On one hand, Zahir Shah, Prime Minister Daud, and ex-Prime Minister Shah Mahmud encouraged support of the Pashtunistan course. On the other, Foreign Minister Naim and his deputy Aziz worked with the United States and European nations to normalize Pakistani relations.[46] Complicating matters further, the U.S. chargé d'affaires in Afghanistan, John Evarts Horner, wrote that "complete retreat by the Government of Afghanistan from its admittedly unreasonable stand on this issue would represent dangerous loss of prestige to the Kabul Government."[47]

At the onset of the Cold War, the United States was much more interested in pursuing regional security arrangements to check Soviet expansionism than it was in resolving border issues between Afghanistan and Pakistan. In the Middle East and South Asia, those efforts focused on Turkey and Pakistan. As the National Security Council (NSC) framed this discussion in 1954, "The best prospect for creating an indigenous regional defense arrangement in the Near East lies in the concept of the 'northern tier,' which would include Turkey, Pakistan, Iran, and Iraq. The Turkish-Pakistan Pact is the first step in this direction."[48] James S. Lay Jr., executive secretary for the NSC, had noted in a coordinating memorandum that "in determining to extend aid to Iran, Iraq, Pakistan and Turkey, the U.S. has chosen states which are most keenly aware of the threat of Soviet Russia and which are located geographically in the way of possible Soviet aggression."[49] Planners in the United States ignored Afghanistan as part of these regional security arrangements due to indefensible northern territories, lack of economic and defense infrastructure, and political instability.[50]

The Pashtunistan question would remain a key issue in Afghanistan's foreign policy during the 1950s and 1960s. Daniel Balland argued that

Prince Mohammad Naim arriving at the White House in 1948 to present his credentials. U.S. diplomats saw Naim, the king's cousin and Mohammad Daud Khan's brother, as the most pro-American of the senior Afghan officials. *National Archives.*

it "continuously poisoned relations between Afghanistan and Pakistan. It even led to serious tension in 1949–50, 1955, and 1959, each instance leading to a partial blockade of the common boundary and a progressive shift of Afghan foreign trade to new transit outlets."[51] Then, from September 3, 1961, until May 29, 1963, a full-scale Pashtunistan crisis resulted in the severing of diplomatic relations and the closure of the Afghan-Pakistani frontier to traffic in both directions.[52] This action confirmed a pro-Soviet shift in Afghanistan, further entrenching trade dependence and forging military ties that would constrain Afghanistan's relationship with the United States and Europe until the end of the twentieth century.

FOUR

Afghanistan's Soviet Shift and the U.S. Response

Afghanistan's move to closer relations with the Soviet Union was a long time coming. Prince Mohammad Naim, then deputy prime minister and minister for foreign affairs, argued in 1954 that "the sending of military aid from the U.S. to Pakistan had created an immediate Soviet reaction and the resulting situation presented one of the chief difficulties faced by Afghanistan today."[1] One of the opening gambits by the Soviets involved oil drilling in northern Afghanistan. In August 1952, the Soviet chargé d'affaires at Kabul delivered an *aide-mémoire* to the Afghan government stating that the Afghan plan to allow a French firm, under the auspices of the United Nations, to pursue oil drilling in northern Afghanistan was a violation of the Afghan-Soviet Neutrality and Non-Aggression Treaty of 1931. The Soviets protested that these explorations by a North Atlantic Treaty Organization (NATO) member would endanger the safety of the Soviet-Afghan frontier and undermine friendly relations between the Soviet Union and Afghanistan.[2]

Initially, the Afghan government rejected the protest, but it later yielded to Soviet pressure and canceled the French project when it became clear that the United States would not increase aid to offset any potential impact on Soviet trade. John Evarts Horner, first secretary and consul at the U.S. embassy in Afghanistan, voiced timely concerns in October 1952 that the State Department "seriously underestimates present and future potentialities [of Soviet] pressure on this country, and utterly neglects regional aspects. Further, no account seems to have been taken of Afghan psychology or existence of important elements here willing to come to terms with [the Soviets]."[3]

As a hedge against Soviet influence in the early 1950s, U.S. officials focused on diplomacy and aid projects in Afghanistan.[4] Horner suggested a "Kabul-Kandahar Road and assistance to Afghan Air Force towards purchase of and facilities for medium transport aircraft which would provide regular government air service to [northern Afghanistan from Kandahar] and at [the] same time greatly strengthen government military strength as against subversion and tribal uprising without giving justifiable cause for alarm to either Pakistan or Soviets."[5] While U.S. officials quickly moved to fill the British void in southwest Asia and expanded economic and military ties with Turkey, Iran, and Pakistan, Afghanistan was largely left out of that process.[6] The Cold War context here was important; notably, the National Intelligence Estimate, "Outlook for Afghanistan," for October 1954 indicated that "Soviet economic penetration may well result in a gradual shift of Afghanistan toward the Soviet orbit. . . . However, we do not believe that the USSR will actually gain control of Afghanistan at least within the next few years."[7]

In December 1953, Vice President Richard M. Nixon and his wife, Patricia, visited Afghanistan. Upon his return, Nixon asserted, "I feel that Afghanistan will stand up against the communists." He noted that he had discussed the Pakistan aid problem with the prime minister and the king, "who suggested that it would be a good idea if Pakistan, Afghanistan, Iraq, Iran, and Turkey entered into something like an 'Atlantic alliance,' with aid going to these countries as a group instead of individually where they might be a threat to each other." Not surprisingly, "The Pakistanis had the opposite view."[8]

U.S. ambassador Henry A. Byroade later observed that "the cold war, as seen from Afghanistan, is only a metamorphosis of an older pattern of conflict." Anglo-Russian competition, which had created a balance of power in South Asia, became more complex by the mid-twentieth century with Iranian, Pakistani, Soviet, British, and American interests competing for shifting sands. Byroade added a further dimension to the question of Afghanistan's development: "Some of the most traditionalist Afghans probably would be willing to go on paying the price of underdevelopment in return for a kind of cocoon-like independence behind mountainous barriers."[9]

The same National Intelligence Estimate of October 1954 offered a sobering account of the increasing Soviet economic pressure on Afghanistan caused by the lack of foreign trade and economic development, as well as by a desire to counter U.S. strategic gains in South Asia and the Middle East. Rather than showing indifference to or ignorance of Afghanistan, the U.S. intelligence review anticipated Afghanistan's lasting quandary:

> Afghan leaders will attempt to obtain additional Western economic aid to counterbalance that received from the USSR and will probably display continuing interest in the idea of participating in Western-backed military aid programs. However, it is unlikely that the Afghans would actually accept membership in a Western-backed area defense arrangement since they could almost certainly realize that

40

Vice President Richard M. Nixon (*right*), **who visited Afghanistan in 1953, showed Prime Minister Mohammad Daud Khan around Washington in 1958. Daud sought aid for his country from the Soviet Union while also continuing to try to maintain good relations with the United States.** *National Archives.*

no foreseeable arrangement could furnish them sufficiently realistic protection against Soviet attack to compensate for the increased hostility toward them which would almost certainly ensue.[10]

A new generation of Afghan leaders came to power while their country confronted the emerging Cold War competition and marched slowly toward modernization.[11] Mohammad Daud Khan replaced Shah Mahmud Khan as prime minister in 1953 and ended the supremacy of Mohammad Zahir Shah's uncles. Daud, a former army general, was well connected with the military: he had been commander of the Kabul Army Corps, minister of war, minister of the interior, and commander of the Central Forces (Quwar-i-Markazi). In addition to his support for rapid modernization and economic development, Daud was a Pashtun nationalist and key advocate for Pashtunistan.[12] As minister of war in the late 1940s, Daud had prepared Afghanistan's request for U.S. arms that had been rejected. Although he preferred to work with the Americans, he had no trouble turning to the Soviets with a similar appeal in the mid-1950s.

A series of events in March 1955 that came to be known as the "Flag Incident" provided the stimulus for deeper Afghan-Soviet ties.[13] On March 27, 1955, Pakistan announced a reorganization of provinces, states, and tribal areas of West Pakistan into one unit. Daud denounced the move, which undermined the autonomy of the frontier provinces. Three days later, an Afghan mob invaded the Pakistan embassy in Kabul and consulates in Kandahar and Jalalabad and burned the Pakistani flags. Pakistani groups responded on April 1, attacking the Afghan consulates in Peshawar and Quetta. The violence forced yet another closure of the border between Afghanistan and Pakistan.[14]

Pakistani leaders ignored any trade implications and used the crisis to advocate with U.S. diplomats for the removal of Daud from power.[15] The United States, however, encouraged Pakistan to open its borders since U.S. aid to Afghanistan depended on this access. U.S. officials correctly feared that decreased aid and curtailed trade through Pakistan would result in increased requests from Afghanistan for Soviet assistance. When Pakistan joined two U.S. security alliances—the Southeast Asia Treaty Organization (SEATO) in September 1954 and the Central Treaty Organization (CENTO) in 1955—Daud approached the Soviet Union for military hardware. He convened a *loya jirga* on November 15, 1955, to support self-determination in Pashtunistan and to accept Soviet military support.[16] Ignoring their own contributions to the crisis, Pakistani leaders blamed the United States when Afghanistan turned to the Soviet Union.

On December 19, 1955, Nikita S. Khrushchev, first secretary of the Communist Party of the Soviet Union, and Nikolai A. Bulganin, premier of the Soviet Union, concluded a five-day visit to Kabul with the offer of a $100 million loan for Afghan development.[17] This loan included credits for building hydroelectric plants, industrial complexes, irrigation projects, modern airports, and a highway system north to the Soviet border. It was the Soviet Union's first major postwar economic agreement and the largest loan outside the Warsaw Pact at the time. From Khrushchev's perspective,

42

The Salang Tunnel, two miles above sea level through the Hindu Kush, connects Afghanistan with Central Asia. It was built with the Soviet aid that started in 1955, with the tunnel opening in 1964. In this 2002 image of the Baghlan Province entrance, an abandoned Soviet IMR combat engineering vehicle can be seen to the left. Photo by Sgt. Todd M. Roy, USA. *Department of Defense.*

"The amount of money we spent in gratuitous assistance to Afghanistan is a drop in the ocean compared with the price we would have had to pay in order to counter the threat of an American military base on Afghan territory."[18] The Soviets also renewed the 1931 Soviet-Afghan Treaty of Non-Aggression and agreed to supply equipment to the Afghan military.

While the United States focused on agricultural and irrigation projects in Afghanistan, the Soviets built long-term strategic infrastructure, including hardened all-weather highways, airports, and airstrips, and expanded ports along the Amu Darya. Khrushchev later noted that the highways that the Soviets built for Afghanistan in the 1950s and 1960s were designed for Soviet military transport and supply "in the case of war with Iran or Pakistan."[19] The Salang Tunnel, along the highway north from Kabul through the Hindu Kush to Termez, and Bagram air base north of Kabul were, and continue to be, particularly important for strategic and commercial reasons.

Afghanistan was the second nonaligned nation after Egypt to receive Soviet arms. From 1955 to 1979, the Soviet Union sent Afghanistan more than $1.25 billion in military aid.[20] The first arms deal between Afghanistan and the Soviet Union, a $3 million sale of Czechoslovak weapons, occurred in mid-1955. In August 1956, Daud accepted a further $32.4 million in Soviet military aid, repayable in cotton, wool, and oilseed. From October 1956 until the end of 1958, the Afghan military received one Il–14 cargo plane, three Il–28 bombers, six MiG–15 and seven MiG–17 fighters, ten Yak–11 and six Yak–18 trainers, ten An–2 utility aircraft, six Mi–1 helicopters, twenty-five T–34 tanks, mobile radios, and small arms.[21]

Along with the equipment, the Soviet military provided technical training and weekly courses in Marxism-Leninism to more than 4,000 Afghan officers between 1956 and 1978.[22] One observer in the 1960s noted that the Afghan armed forces had "become almost completely dependent upon the Soviets, not only for equipment but also for logistic support."[23] This support included deliveries of gasoline, ammunition, and spare parts, giving the Soviets control over Afghan military operations. The Soviet military had particular influence over the Royal Afghan Air Force because of its dependence on Soviet-bloc aircraft and advisors. Most Afghan air crews also trained in the Soviet Union.[24]

The military and economic modernization enabled by the Soviets was complemented by Soviet support on the controversial Pashtunistan issue. Following his 1955 visit, Khrushchev recommended that "the Pushtun people should decide by a free plebiscite whether they want to remain within the borders of Pakistan, to form a new and independent state, or to unite with Afghanistan."[25] A 1956 National Intelligence Estimate stated that Daud's acceptance of extensive Soviet aid "is motivated by his desire to strengthen Afghanistan in its controversy with Pakistan over the Pushtunistan issue and also to develop Afghanistan economically." The authors continued, "Daud has won effective support for his policies in the limited circle of potentially significant Afghans, and he is not likely to be ousted in the foreseeable future. So long as he remains in power he will probably continue to seek Soviet aid and support."[26]

U.S. Response

The goodwill built between the United States and Afghanistan during World War II by Cornelius Van H. Engert was quickly lost during the Cold War. In the 1956 National Intelligence Estimate cited above, U.S. intelligence analysts identified the need to increase aid to counter the growing Soviet presence.[27] Ambassador Sheldon T. Mills suggested a further corrective in 1958: "During the past two years our economic aid policy with respect to Afghanistan has been formulated as [a] reaction to Soviet policy. What we are suggesting is that at that crossroads in Afghanistan's history we reach positively, rather than drift and have our next major policy decision with respect to Afghanistan come as [a] reaction to some Russian move."[28] Throughout the postwar era, U.S.

Capt. Everett W. Wood (*left*), the Pan American/Ariana instructor, presents pilot stripes to Enaam-ul-Haq Gran, the first Afghan to complete training to fly for Ariana Airlines. The U.S. signed an agreement in 1956 for Pan Am to provide training and assistance, and Pan Am ultimately purchased a significant stake in Ariana. *National Archives.*

officials rejected Afghan requests for military aid and displayed favoritism toward pro-western Pakistan and Iran, both of which Afghanistan viewed as rivals. While U.S. aid finally arrived in the 1950s, U.S. planners did not focus on intrinsic strategic interests in Afghanistan, but rather on limiting Soviet efforts there.[29]

One of the challenges faced by U.S. aid officials in competing with the Soviets was their different approach to financing assistance projects. The Soviets funded their projects on credits that created long-term economic dependence for Afghanistan, and they offered small investments with immediate dividends.[30] U.S. aid programs, on the other hand, supported long-term development in education and the massive Helmand Valley project (discussed in chapter 5), which was chronically underfunded and slowed by Pakistani blockades. Thus Afghans recognized the new Soviet-funded roads and military hardware more easily than the intangible benefits that the U.S.-backed initiatives would offer in the future. Ambassador Byroade observed in 1961 that "the delays in some of these projects have been such as to cause many an Afghan to question the whole policy of the United States toward their country." Noting the disparity of development

American Jane Williams teaching at the Rabia-e Balkhi Girls High School in Kabul around 1960. She was there as part of a U.S. government-sponsored program run by Columbia University's Teachers College, which administered it from 1954 to 1978. The school was almost totally destroyed during the civil war period but was rebuilt in the 2000s. As of this writing, it has nearly 4,000 students. *National Archives.*

in areas assisted by the United States and the Soviet Union, Byroade added the warning that "Afghanistan is a sort of 'economic Korea.'"[31]

In the first rounds of funding, the U.S. government extended aid through the Export-Import Bank of $21 million on November 23, 1949, and $18.5 million on May 4, 1954, under President Harry S. Truman's Mutual Security Program.[32] This cash infusion supported a variety of programs, including Helmand Valley agricultural projects, transportation and road projects, language and technical education, and wheat purchases from U.S. farmers. Through the end of the 1950s and peaking in the mid-1960s, the U.S. government invested heavily in two ventures in southern Afghanistan that did not generate returns: one involved civil aviation and the expansion of the Kandahar airport, and the other continued funding for an extensive hydroelectric and irrigation project in the Helmand Valley.

On June 23, 1956, U.S. ambassador Mills and Afghan foreign minister Naim signed an agreement in Kabul for $14.5 million to fund the construction of Kandahar International Airport and to formalize an agreement for Pan American World Airways to offer training and operational assistance.[33]

Pan American would ultimately purchase 49 percent of the Afghan Ariana Airline through this arrangement and participate in goodwill exercises that transported Afghan pilgrims during the annual hajj.[34] The International Cooperation Administration (ICA) allocated these funds "to give Afghanistan a fast and economical air transportation system which is particularly suitable to the country."[35] The plan was to curb Afghanistan's aviation dependence on the Soviet Union by expanding domestic air service and building new airports to support it. Kandahar International Airport was completed in March 1960, but the world-class facility was soon bypassed by jet aircraft that could fly directly from Europe to South Asia without a stopover.[36] In addition to its financial assistance, ICA also helped Ariana Airline acquire a DC–6B passenger aircraft, its sixth Douglas aircraft, on May 2, 1960. The aircraft flew from Washington, DC, National Airport to Newark, New Jersey, and then to Afghanistan in time to support the hajj.[37]

PRESIDENT EISENHOWER'S VISIT TO AFGHANISTAN

In the late 1950s, Zahir Shah intensified his diplomatic profile in the world and promoted his *bi-tarafi* (literally "without sides," or nonaligned) philosophy.[38] As he stated during Afghan Independence Day celebrations in 1957, "The country's foreign policy is based on the continued safeguarding

President Dwight D. Eisenhower received a royal welcome at Bagram air field in December 1959. Dignitaries included the king, Mohammad Zahir Shah (*right of Eisenhower*), and Prime Minister Mohammad Daud Khan (*far left*). Photo by Sultan Hamid. *Eisenhower Presidential Library.*

Thousands of Afghans lined the roads to see the motorcade that carried President Eisenhower into Kabul. He later wrote that "I was heartened to see such spirit in people of whose sympathies we had been doubtful." Photo by Thomas J. O'Halloran. *Library of Congress.*

and strengthening of good relations with friendly States. Efforts are being made to establish and strengthen these ties with all the peoples and nations of the world."[39] He then embarked on a two-year campaign to engage U.S. leaders at the highest level of government and demonstrate Afghanistan's political and economic independence from the Soviet Union.[40]

As part of this initiative, Prime Minister Daud visited the United States as an "official guest" of the government from June 24 to 27, 1958.[41] During one of their meetings, Secretary of State John Foster Dulles expressed that he understood the motives that led Afghanistan to accept Soviet assistance, mentioning specifically "the fact that Afghanistan is a land-locked country and its transit difficulties with Pakistan naturally led Afghanistan to seek a route for its commerce to the north."[42] Meetings focused on affirming Afghanistan's "independence" while seeking additional ways the United States could support Afghanistan's economic development projects.

A little over a year later, President Dwight D. Eisenhower returned the favor of a state visit when he landed at Bagram air field and remained in Kabul for six hours on December 9, 1959, as part of his "Flight to Peace" goodwill tour of eleven nations.[43] This trip was the first official use of Air Force One, the new VC–137 aircraft, and this stop was the first presidential visit to Afghanistan.[44] Upon his arrival, Eisenhower addressed the crowd "to convey the warm and friendly greetings of the American people to Afghanistan and its people."[45] During a luncheon at Chilstoon Palace, Eisenhower underlined the two countries' shared values of peace and prosperity, adding that "most importantly, we share with the Afghan people a sense of the great spiritual values deriving from our respective religious heritages. We are drawn together in devotion to the abiding values of religion."[46] As they had during Daud's visit to the United States, public pleasantries abounded, while meetings focused on confirming Afghanistan's neutrality and finding ways to maintain U.S. financial commitment to Afghanistan.[47]

Of note, Eisenhower recalled his concern when Air Force One was first "accompanied by Russian-built MIGs—part of the Afghan Air Force" in Afghan air space, adding that "our pleasure in our reception was dampened by the presence of MIG aircraft on the field."[48] Yet the genuine outpouring of goodwill from the Afghan people surprised Eisenhower:

> [We] experienced for the first time in the tour the excitement of a mob bursting out of control. Suddenly, and without warning, we found our vehicles unable to move, almost sinking in a sea of strange faces. But the faces were friendly in spite of the inconvenience and unavoidable delay; I was heartened to see such a spirit in people of whose sympathies we had been doubtful.[49]

Soviet-built Bagram air field during President Eisenhower's visit, with Soviet-provided MiG–15s to the left and Il–28 bombers to the right. Photo by Thomas J. O'Halloran. *Library of Congress.*

After his visit to Kabul, Eisenhower privately expressed his reservations about Soviet influence in Afghanistan. According to the record of a conversation between Eisenhower and Spanish head of state Francisco Franco in late December 1959,

> The Afghans say that they can remain independent and that their purpose is to remain neutral. The President doesn't see how this can be done, for while the royal family may continue to stay on in power, the Soviets are gradually bringing roads through and around the country and through other construction are also getting more and more of a grip on the nation and in time the President thought it would be likely to become Soviet dominated.[50]

FIVE

The Helmand River Valley Project and the Pakistan Question

Far and away the most substantial U.S. involvement in Afghanistan from the end of World War II until the Soviet invasion in 1979, with a particular emphasis in the 1950s, was with various projects intended to develop the Helmand River Valley in the southern half of the country. The Helmand River is the largest in Afghanistan, providing 40 percent of the country's water resources. The Arghandab River serves as the major tributary to the west and continues to the Sistan Basin. Adequate water has never been an issue for the Helmand River Valley; however, the inability to properly control and distribute the river's resources has plagued the region for centuries.[1]

In 1910, Afghans began work to reconstruct irrigation canals around Seraj, south of Musa Qala, that dated back several centuries. Engineers completed the first functional canals by 1914. In the 1930s, Germany and Japan provided technical assistance for additional improvements. The Japanese built nine miles of new canals at Boghra from 1937 to 1941. During the war, Dr. S. W. Shah, a Cornell University-educated Afghan engineer, led the expansion to twenty-five miles.[2]

When the war ended and its German and Japanese partners were gone, the Afghan government turned to the United States for assistance. Due to the strength of its trade in wool during the war, Afghanistan had accumulated a $20 million trade surplus and allocated $17 million to agricultural development plans in the Helmand and Arghandab River Valleys.[3]

In 1945, the Afghan government began negotiations with Morrison-Knudsen, the U.S. construction company that had built the Hoover (Boulder) Dam, to build two diversion dams, one on the Helmand River and the other on the Arghandab River, and to improve the irrigation canals and roads in both areas. They reached an agreement in 1946, forming Morrison-Knudsen Afghanistan (MKA), headquartered in San Francisco, California. The Morrison-Knudsen dams were the first major U.S. development projects in Afghanistan, and the overall Helmand River Valley project remains the largest single aid endeavor there to date.[4] Prime

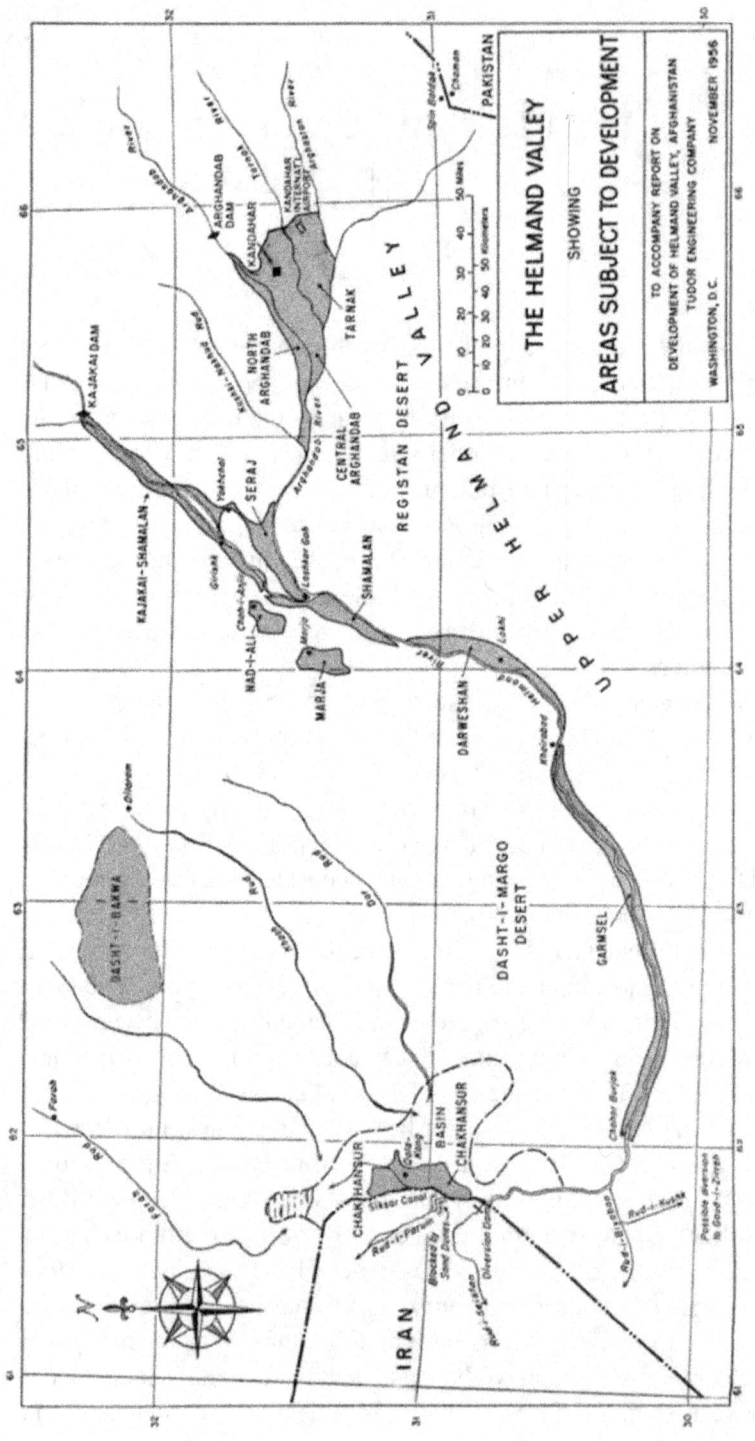

THE HELMAND VALLEY

SHOWING

AREAS SUBJECT TO DEVELOPMENT

TO ACCOMPANY REPORT ON

DEVELOPMENT OF HELMAND VALLEY, AFGHANISTAN

TUDOR ENGINEERING COMPANY

WASHINGTON, D.C.   NOVEMBER 1956

This map from *Report on Development of Helmand Valley, Afghanistan* (1956) shows the project as it was envisioned; the lower section below Khairobad was never completed. The Kajakai Dam on the Helmand River is in the upper right, and the Arghandab (Dahla) Dam on the Arghandab River is about twenty miles north of Kandahar. From early in the project in the late 1940s, Iran claimed that the development was reducing the amount of water it received via the Helmand River, a dispute that the U.S. mediated for two decades.

Dahla Dam on the Arghandab River north of Kandahar was completed in 1952 and originally known as the Arghandab Dam. It was built by Morrison-Knudsen Afghanistan, a subsidiary of the American firm that had built the Hoover Dam, among other large-scale projects. Photo (2012) by Mark Ray. *Department of Defense.*

Minister Shah Mahmud Ghazi Khan wrote in 1946: "America's attitude is our salvation. For the first time in our history, we are free of the threat of great powers' using our mountain passes as pathways to empire. Now we can concentrate our talents and resources on bettering the living conditions of our own people." He continued: "I propose to reduce the army in size to that of a small but well-trained internal security force charged with maintaining order among the nomadic tribesmen. Money once used in maintaining a large army will find better use in the already started national improvement program."[5]

The Americans initially envisioned the Helmand project as a replica of the Tennessee Valley Authority (TVA) for Afghanistan that included farms for nomads, agricultural products for export, hydroelectric power, and flood mitigation, all generating revenue to pay for the endeavor. President Harry S. Truman was an enthusiastic supporter of hydroelectric diplomacy in general, advocating for "a TVA in the Yangtze Valley and the Danube."[6] There were, however, problems with the Afghanistan project from early in the process. Ambassador Louis G. Dreyfus Jr. cabled the State Department in September 1949 that "present widespread criticism of [Morrison-Knudson] and American efficiency voiced by [Abdul] Majid [Zabuli] seriously undermining U.S. prestige. For approximately $20,000,000 spent

[the] only tangible returns Afghanistan has are one short road, one diversion dam, and one incomplete canal." Nevertheless, Dreyfus favored approval of a pending Export-Import Bank loan to "avoid reduced U.S. prestige and cooling of present cordial Afghan-U.S. relations."[7]

On February 11, 1949, the Afghan economic mission to the United States had requested $55 million from the Export-Import Bank of the United States to finance Helmand Valley development. Minister Abdul Majid Zabuli, a successful businessman in Afghanistan, insisted that the development plan represented an integrated series of interdependent agricultural and industrial projects. The Export-Import Bank, however, approved less than half the requested amount—a $21 million loan—in November 1949 to fund only MKA's Arghandab, Kajakai, and Boghra canal projects. MKA responded by cutting costs, including ground-water surveys, road paving, and other support projects.[8]

Afghan officials recognized the economic and diplomatic importance of the Helmand Valley initiative and made efforts to fortify it. In 1951, the Afghan government gave more authority to MKA and created the Helmand Valley Authority in December 1952 to oversee the project, elevating the authority to cabinet status.[9] Engineers built the Dahla Dam on the Arghandab River between June 1950 and January 1952 and completed the Kajakai Dam on the Helmand River in April 1953.[10] American and Afghan officials alike were aware of the growing costs: the Afghan government had already spent $95 million by the mid-1950s, with $39.5 million financed by the Export-Import Bank.

Publicly, the United States continued to praise the Afghanistan projects. A State Department *Bulletin* noted in July 1952 that "help in overcoming effects of ravages during the twelfth and fourteenth centuries by Genghis Khan and Tamerlane on vital irrigation works in the Helmand Valley of southwest Afghanistan is among provisions" of the Point Four funds.[11] Maj. Gen. Glen E. Edgerton, USA (ret.), managing director of the Export-Import Bank, said in 1954, speaking of the overall effort, that "this great project constitutes a basic feature of the economic development program of Afghanistan and, when completed, will stand as an enduring monument to the enterprise of the Afghan people and to the friendship and cooperation of Afghanistan and the United States."[12]

Out of public view, however, concerns grew. Nearly a year before Edgerton's statement praising the project, a report to the Export-Import Bank noted that the effort was underfunded for the scale of the endeavor and hindered by Pakistani border politics and low educational levels of the Afghans it would employ and eventually benefit. According to the report, both locals and U.S. aid groups experienced a cultural disconnect

Kajakai Dam, on the Helmand River, is the largest dam in Afghanistan. It was completed in 1953 by Morrison-Knudsen Afghanistan. USAID began installing hydroelectric power stations in 1975, units that became U.S. bombing targets in 2001. They were subsequently restored, and development efforts on and associated with the dam have been a major focus in the 2000s. It is shown from the reservoir side in a 2012 image, with the spillway to the right. Photo by Mark Ray. *Department of Defense.*

and could not overcome a lack of appreciation of this "America in Asia" project.[13]

There were also U.S. concerns that "the failure of the project for any reason would be a severe blow to American prestige and American relations in this part of the world," as one official put it in 1953.[14] Secretary of State John Foster Dulles cabled the embassy in Pakistan in 1955 that the "Morrison-Knudsen Corporation activities in Afghanistan must be discontinued in [the] near future if [Pakistan's] embargo of their shipments continues. This company is one of [the] chief influences which maintains Afghan connections with [the] West. Its departure would create [a] vacuum which [the] Soviets would be anxious to fill."[15]

In a report published in 1955, economist Peter G. Franck noted that although a United Nations preparatory mission had "recommended that the UN provide assistance to Helmand Valley projects already started, UN headquarters entertained doubts about the economic soundness of the projects proposed and the Government's administrative capacity to complete them." As Louis Dupree observed, "Neither the Afghan government nor the American engineering company understood the monumental problems of

Mohammad Kabir Ludin, Afghan ambassador to the United States, signs documents for an $18.5 million loan from the Export-Import Bank of the United States in May 1954. Maj. Gen. Glen E. Edgerton, USA (ret.), managing director of the bank, looks on. Photo by Joseph O'Donnell. *National Archives.*

enfolding an entire region in the embrace of a single project."[16] Infrastructure and local interest were almost entirely absent. Costs quickly escalated, and officials realized how difficult it was to ship U.S. equipment halfway around the world, with Pakistan hindering deliveries through transit fees and closed borders.

A Tudor Engineering Report that evaluated the Helmand River Valley project in 1956 anticipated added income to the Afghan economy from the increase in arable land. One State Department official noted that "the project is using the waters of the Helmand River to irrigate lands some of which have not been extensively cultivated in more than 2,000 years. It also includes industry, power, and transportation features."[17] But hoped-for revenues that would eventually make the project self-sustaining and profitable never materialized. Indeed, in a later study, economist Nake M. Kamrany found "no signs of its financial liquidity."[18]

In the later 1950s, the Afghan Ministry of Interior funded the development of villages around Nad-e Ali in Helmand Province to settle Pashtun, Uzbek, and Baluch nomads. But the logistics and impact of resettling the local nomadic population were not well considered. These problems, combined with poor soil conditions, led to the new villages being abandoned by 1960.[19]

There were other issues as the project developed. Geographer Aloys A. Michel observed in the late 1950s that "United States interest centers on the Helmand Valley and has, wittingly or not, taken the position of favoring Kandahar over Kabul as the transportation and commercial center of the nation." He cautioned that this stance "ultimately is untenable, for the Durrani Afghans long ago decided, despite their personal attachment to the South, that the only way to rule Afghanistan was from Kabul."[20]

In a concluding observation in his 1959 work, Michel stated that "at present the ICA [U.S. International Cooperation Administration] agricultural program in the Helmand [Valley] has practically collapsed, and no amount of United States Government support for the Kandahar International Airport or Industrial Center or for Arghandab power can offset the damage done to American prestige by the failures in Nad-i-Ali."[21] Kamrany later noted that "of the seven major objectives of the project, . . . only one objective was successfully accomplished, i.e., the project provided protection against floods; but at a very high cost!"[22]

The Afghan government released Morrison-Knudsen from its contract in 1959, with recriminations on both sides. As Ambassador Henry A. Byroade observed:

> I am normally against a proliferation of projects, and feel that a few big projects are better in the long run than a scattering of effort. This is an unusual situation, however, and if we can double our effect here by new things with a bit of flair, then it seems we should do so. The new Minister of Agriculture stated we were putting too many eggs in one basket in the Helmand Valley and that there was a feeling that too many of our subsequent projects had been designed simply to make that successful.[23]

Major U.S. investments in the Helmand and Arghandab River projects continued into the 1970s, despite the lack of infrastructure, the diplomatic challenges of Pashtunistan, and a growing awareness of opium poppy cultivation in the region. "While the concept of the Helmand Valley development is basically Afghan," Ambassador Byroade explained in 1961, "U.S. financing and the employment of a U.S. contractor by the Afghans have tended to identify the United States closely with it." Even into the 1960s, American officials held onto the idea that the "most effective instrument available to maintain an effective U.S. position in Afghanistan is our aid program."[24] But the ongoing struggles and financial burdens of the project imperiled U.S. influence.

The Pakistan Question

When the Afghan government accepted massive Soviet funding for development projects during the 1950s, Afghan officials cited U.S. support of Pakistan as a major factor in its decision.[25] The Afghan government was so concerned with Pakistan's growing military strength that it even began funding its defense at the expense of agricultural programs, which resulted in poor decisions on the Helmand River Valley project and a new reliance on U.S. wheat imports to feed its people.[26] Despite this assistance, U.S. support for Pakistan continued to plague its relationship with Afghanistan.[27]

U.S. officials were aware that prosperity in Afghanistan relied on a partnership with Pakistan. A National Security Council assessment in 1957 reported that "Afghanistan has already incurred so heavy a burden of debt to the Communist bloc as to threaten its future independence," noting that the Afghans were also "willing to accept Western assistance and technical advice and hope to have the best of both worlds." The United States wanted to assist "the improvement of communications through Pakistan to Afghanistan, to bring about closer and more amicable Afghan-Pakistan relations and also give Afghanistan an alternative to its dependence on the USSR." The desire was to "encourage Afghanistan to minimize its reliance upon the Communist bloc for military training and equipment, and to look to the United States and other free world sources for military training and assistance."[28]

The following year, however, Afghan-Pakistani relations further deteriorated. While Pakistani president Iskander A. Mirza had presided over a détente on the Pashtunistan issue, Gen. Muhammad Ayub Khan reignited tension when he seized power in Pakistan in October 1958. Ayub Khan, himself an ethnic Pashtun of the Tarin tribe, demanded that Afghanistan yield on the Pashtunistan issue. That was not going to happen with Mohammad Daud Khan as Afghanistan's prime minister. As his brother the foreign minister, Mohammad Naim Khan, explained to Dwight D. Eisenhower during the president's brief visit in 1959, the Pashtunistan dispute "had deep roots in history and in the mentality and emotions of the people; anything that went wrong in Pushtun Pakistan reacted strongly here, causing bitterness, tenseness and difficulties in their relations."[29]

When Nikita S. Khrushchev, then premier of the Soviet Union, visited Afghanistan in early March 1960, he supported Afghanistan's position on Pashtunistan and reiterated the Soviet desire for a plebiscite in Pakistan's tribal regions to determine their future.[30] On September 23, 1960, the U.S. embassy in Kabul reported a "threatening situation" in Bajaur, Pakistan,

Soviet leader Nikita S. Khrushchev at a meeting of the United Nations General Assembly in New York, September 1960. His open support of Afghanistan on the Pashtunistan issue created challenges for the United States in its relations with both Afghanistan and Pakistan. Photo by Warren K. Leffler. *Library of Congress.*

where pro-Afghan and pro-Pakistan groups had escalated hostilities. Prime Minister Daud met with Ambassador Byroade and indicated that Afghanistan would be forced to protect local tribes if Pakistani troops quelled the violence.[31] From the Afghan point of view, the Durand Line was not an issue since local tribes did not observe the international boundary of Afghanistan and Pakistan. Instead, Daud focused discussion on the fact that Afghanistan supported Pashtun tribes irrespective of their location.[32] A month later, President Eisenhower informed Mohammad Zahir Shah that the United States would not mediate and expressed hope that Afghanistan and Pakistan would engage in bilateral negotiations to resolve their conflicts.[33] The Soviets exacerbated the situation again in March 1961 when Khrushchev publicly declared that "Pushtunistan has always been part of Afghanistan."[34] Tensions continued to mount until September 3, 1961, when Afghanistan closed its border and Pakistan shut Afghanistan's consulates. The borders remained closed until May 29, 1963.

While U.S. officials hoped to mediate the Afghan-Pakistan dispute, they were hindered by their position as Pakistan's ally.[35] Importantly for broader U.S. strategic interests, Eisenhower had reached an agreement with Pakistani prime minister Huseyn Shaheed Suhrawardy in 1957 to

A dixieland combo of the U.S. Air Forces in Europe Band's Ambassadors jazz ensemble plays outside the mausoleum of Abdur Rahman Khan in Kabul in 1968. The group was in Afghanistan to perform at the Jeshyn Fair, an event celebrating that country's independence. *USAF in Europe Band.*

build a secret base for U–2 aircraft, located at the Peshawar Air Station in Badaber, Pakistan.[36] The base was also used by the 6937th Communications Group, U.S. Air Force Security Service, for a communications link between Karamursel, Turkey, and Peshawar, Pakistan.[37] Understanding the importance of the U–2 base in Peshawar to the United States, Pakistani officials leveraged the issue.[38] According to one analysis in 1964, "The

Prime Minister Mohammad Hashim Maiwandwal of Afghanistan in Washington, DC, in 1967 at the White House with President Lyndon B. Johnson. Photo by Yoichi Okamoto. *Johnson Presidential Library.*

Pakistani President knows that the strongest card he holds is the U.S. communications facilities at Peshawar. . . . He almost certainly calculates that closing the facilities would bring a drastic reduction in the U.S. military and economic assistance on which Pakistan is so heavily dependent and for which there is no alternative in sight."[39] At the same time, the border closing placed increased pressure on U.S. aid programs to Afghanistan. The Afghan government requested an alternate transportation route through Iran, but the United States preferred the less costly passage through Pakistan and decided to wait. U.S. policy makers continued to make their Afghanistan policy conditional upon improved relations with Pakistan and hoped for a resolution to the differences.

In the end, the solution arose in Afghanistan. The closed borders wreaked havoc on the Afghan economy, and mediation to open them was slow and arduous. The royal family, fearful of Daud's pro-Soviet policies and autocratic rule, had been moving toward his removal. Zahir Shah asked Daud to step down as prime minister, and Daud resigned on March 10, 1963. Mohammad Yusuf, a physicist, became the new prime minister (1963–65), followed by Mohammad Hashim Maiwandwal (1965–67). They led Afghanistan toward a more cosmopolitan society and a constitutional monarchy. They also improved relations with Pakistan, and the Pashtunistan issue was sidelined until the mid-1970s.

*   *   *

Outwardly, Afghanistan enjoyed a relatively stable period in the 1960s and the early 1970s as world leaders focused their Cold War attentions elsewhere. When President Lyndon B. Johnson invited Prime Minister Maiwandwal to Washington in March 1967, he remarked: "Historically, the relations between our countries have been close and cordial. Today they are warmer than ever before." Unquestionably, the Afghan-U.S. relationship continued to focus on development aid. Prime Minister Maiwandwal specifically noted in his reply Afghanistan's appreciation for American help "in building our infrastructure," mentioning the Kabul-Kandahar highway and another under construction. He also highlighted U.S. help developing "our educational systems, our agriculture, our water resources, and our transportation system."[40]

From the late 1940s until the late 1970s, Afghan officials balanced Cold War competition in Afghanistan.[41] As Daud once quipped, "I feel the happiest when I can light my American cigarette with Soviet matches."[42] However, a new and increasingly unstable period began on July 17, 1973, when Daud overthrew Zahir Shah in a nearly bloodless coup d'état while the king was abroad for medical treatment.[43] Daud abolished the monarchy and declared himself the first president of Afghanistan. Pakistan, playing on fears of Soviet influence in Afghanistan and concerned about a return of the Pashtunistan debate, immediately pressed the United States for more military aid.[44] In fact, following Daud's return to power, he was much more moderate on the Pashtunistan question than he had been during his previous rule and more focused on modernization. As Amin Saikal explained, Daud's intentions "were two-fold: to reduce his dependence on local communists and the Soviet Union as well as military expenditure, and expand economic and trade ties with Pakistan."[45] By the mid-1970s, Afghanistan's relationships with Pakistan and Iran had greatly improved. But Daud gradually lost control of relations with the Soviets, ultimately with devastating results.

SIX

Socialist Afghanistan and War with the Soviet Union

In the 1950s and 1960s, Soviet scholars developed a concept of a native "military intelligentsia" to confront the weakness of socialist revolutionary movements in developing nations.[1] In Afghanistan, Soviet planners hoped this new military elite would assume leadership positions in future national movements. Accordingly, the socialist People's Democratic Party of Afghanistan (PDPA, Hizb-e-Demokratik-e-Khalq-e-Afghanistan) started actively recruiting Afghan officers trained in the Soviet Union. By the early 1970s, the strategy began to demonstrate success. A communication to Washington from the U.S. embassy in 1971 observed that there was "no effective organization within the military to counter or even catalog the long-term, possibly subversive effects of Soviet training of the many military officers who go to the USSR for stints as long as six years."[2]

In 1973, 1978, and 1979, Soviet-trained officers played pivotal roles in Afghan political change.[3] Without a popular base supporting the leaders, however, the rapid succession of coups led by mid-level officers introduced political disarray in Afghanistan. As foreign minister in 1971 and as prime minister in 1972, Mohammad Musa Shafiq sought reconciliation with Pakistan on the Pashtunistan issue and agreements with Iran on the use of the Helmand River. When Afghanistan suffered a drought in 1972, Iran offered $2 billion in aid over ten years. Soviet leaders quickly responded to the Iranian overture, using their military ties to engineer a coup in 1973 led by former Prime Minister Mohammad Daud Khan and the military. The officers intended Daud to be a figurehead, but he subsequently outmaneuvered and demoted many of them.[4]

After the 1973 coup, the Soviet military increased shipments of equipment, including T–54 and T 55 tanks, Il–28 bombers, armed personnel carriers, and light and medium field artillery pieces.[5] Despite this augmentation in the Afghan military's inventory of arms and equipment, Daud moved to decrease the number of Soviet advisors in Afghanistan. In 1976, he reassigned Soviet advisors from the company to the battalion level.

Daud turned away from the Soviet training monopoly in 1974 when he sent military officers abroad to India and Egypt, nations that also used Soviet weapon systems. Still, Daud never cut military ties with the Soviets, and Afghanistan remained dependent on their hardware and training.[6]

Daud also included PDPA members in his new government, where they continued their strategy of recruiting military officers. At the time, the PDPA was divided between two factions, both with military links. The first of these, Parcham, was dominated by Tajiks, Uzbeks, and Dari-speaking Kabulis. The members of Khalq, its rival, were largely Pashtuns from the provinces. Generally, the Soviet Politburo supported both sides, establishing ties with whichever group prevailed. But the Soviet military apparatus had specific links to each group: Soviet military intelligence (GRU) supported Khalq, while the Committee for State Security (KGB) supported Parcham.[7] During the 1970s, Khalq increased its influence within the Afghan military, asserting that military promotions should be based on ability rather than family and tribal connections. Daud, however, returned family members to the military elite. By the late 1970s, despite differences between the two factions, the PDPA became a significant political force.

Daud began more openly eschewing the Soviets in 1978. His domestic economic reforms had proven unsuccessful, and he pursued new support and new regional allies in Iran, Egypt, Pakistan, and China. His seven-year economic plan, outlined for 1976 through 1983, followed Soviet models but was based on massive financial aid from Iran.[8] A new reordering of alliances would not take place, however. As Daud was organizing the visit of the Shah of Iran to Kabul and his own visit to Washington, a series of events led to another coup, his own downfall, and the preservation of Soviet ties.

Unrest at the funeral of Parcham activist Mir Akbar Khyber sparked massive demonstrations and a confounding series of events in Kabul. Shocked by the power of the socialist movement, Daud ordered the arrests of PDPA leaders Nur Muhammad Taraki, Hafizullah Amin, and Babrak Karmal. On April 27, 1978, Amin, who was merely under house arrest, ordered army officers loyal to the Khalq faction to initiate a coup d'état, later known as the Saur Revolution.[9] At seven o'clock on the evening of April 27, Col. Abdul Qadir Dagarwal, a Soviet-trained pilot, announced in Dari and Mohammad Aslam Watanjar in Pashto on Radio Afghanistan that a revolutionary council of the armed forces would replace the Daud government.[10] Only the 7th Division at Rishkor, the 15th Armored Brigade, and the Republican Guard remained loyal to Daud.[11] Henry Bradsher, a Pulitzer Prize-winning journalist, observed that "whatever the genesis of

The Soviets built this control tower at Bagram air field in 1976 as their involvement in Afghanistan began to intensify. It was heavily damaged during the civil war, but after U.S. troops took control of the base in late 2001, the U.S. Air Force renovated the facility and used it until a new tower was completed in 2008. The building remained in service, housing Air Force units as part of Camp Cunningham. Photo (2009) by Capt. David Faggard, USAF. *Department of Defense.*

the downfall of [Daud], it was accomplished by a small number of military men . . . at the air base side of Kabul International Airport. Only some 600 men, 60 tanks and 20 warplanes were involved in approximately nineteen hours of rebel action against the more numerous loyalist forces."[12] By the morning of April 28, Daud and his brother Mohammad Naim Khan were dead, and new rulers controlled Kabul.

Examining both Soviet and Afghan sources, Bradsher raised questions about the level of direct Soviet involvement in the coup. The Soviet embassy in Kabul seemed to be as surprised as other embassies, but Soviet leaders acted quickly to publicize their close ties and maintain their record as the first capital to recognize the new Afghan government.[13] U.S. officials hedged in their responses, avoiding terms that would trigger the Foreign Assistance Act of 1961, which prohibited assistance to "any Communist country."[14]

From April 27, 1978, until the Soviet invasion on December 24, 1979, the new Afghan leaders demonstrated little capacity to govern.[15] Rapid economic and social changes, the increasing number of Soviet advisors, and political infighting among Afghan communists led to instability and

Soviet leader Leonid I. Brezhnev (*right*) with President Gerald R. Ford during a summit meeting in Vladivostok, USSR, in November 1974. Brezhnev concluded a treaty with Afghan leaders in December 1978 that closely linked Afghanistan with the Soviet Union. *National Archives.*

greater dependency on the Soviets. On May 1, 1978, Taraki became prime minister, and he promptly carried out a purge of Parcham supporters in the military and the government.[16] Bradsher recorded that "many foreign observers felt that the Communist coup was greeted by most Afghans with relief. . . . Those hopes were quickly shattered."[17]

Taraki established PDPA offices at each level of the Afghan armed forces, and he made Soviet training a requirement for elite units in Kabul. Soviet advisors, newly assigned to the platoon level, proliferated. Soviet advisors numbered 350 in 1977; 2,000 in May 1978; 7,000 in August 1978; and more than 10,000 in December 1979. Soviet advisors could even wear Afghan military uniforms and assume combat and leadership roles in the Afghan National Army.[18]

During the summer of 1978, Moscow officials attempted a low profile in Afghan relations—despite providing $250 million in Soviet weapons to the Afghan army—and focused on developing relations with the PDPA.[19] In news conferences, the PDPA deliberately rejected Soviet ties and communist nomenclature, asserting nonaligned status.[20]

When Taraki visited Moscow from December 4 to 7, 1978, he and Soviet General Secretary Leonid I. Brezhnev signed the "Treaty of Friendship,

Good Neighborliness, and Cooperation" on December 5. Their ties were then undeniable. Article 4 of the treaty underlined the importance of "security, independence, and territorial integrity" and reaffirmed the military connections between the two countries. Although the Soviets did not commit themselves to prevent the downfall of the PDPA, many have argued that this treaty effectively established Afghanistan as a Soviet satellite. With Soviet support secured, Afghan leaders then embarked on a campaign of arrests of secular and religious leaders not aligned with the new regime. Prisons grew overcrowded, and there was a surge of executions.[21]

Journalist Edward Girardet described the administrative inexperience of the new Afghan cabinet members, observing that "most of them had been lower or middle rank civil servants." He added that "it was even worse in the provinces, where those who took control of government offices had few if any qualifications whatsoever. Many were quite simply ignorant thugs or opportunists who used their newly acquired positions to improve their social standing, settle old rivalries, or feather their nests through self-bestowed privileges and bribes."[22]

The year 1979 proved pivotal for U.S. interests in Afghanistan. On February 14, four armed militants kidnapped the U.S. ambassador, Adolph "Spike" Dubs, and demanded the release of imprisoned members of the National Oppression Party (Settem-e Melli) in exchange. The Afghan government refused negotiations, then organized a rescue attempt by Afghan police and Soviet security force advisors that failed and resulted in the death of Ambassador Dubs.[23]

U.S.-Afghan relations quickly deteriorated following the "Dubs Affair." Publicly, Harold H. Saunders, the assistant secretary of state for near east affairs, testified to Congress: "For its part, the U.S. Government seeks no special position in Afghanistan. We look for a relationship based on mutual respect and shared interests in regional stability, the independence and territorial integrity of all states in the area, and nonintervention."[24] President James E. Carter Jr. curtailed aid programs that were impossible to fulfill with the growing unrest, withdrew aid workers who could not be protected, and began providing radio equipment, medical supplies, and money to the Afghan resistance movement.[25] President Ronald W. Reagan continued and later expanded this assistance after he took office in 1981.[26]

In the face of unforgiving land reforms and government interference in daily life dictated by the new socialist government, popular armed resistance burgeoned, starting in Nuristan and Badakhshan. Similar revolts followed in Paktia, Paktika, Ningrahar, Kapisa, Uruzgan, Parwan, Badghis, Balkh, Ghazni, Farah, and Herat. In March 1979, Capt. Ismail

Tajbeg Palace, on a hillside overlooking Kabul. The Soviets stormed it in December 1979 and killed Afghan president Hafizullah Amin. The structure became the staff headquarters for the Soviet Fortieth Army during the occupation. Also known as the Queen's Palace, it was built in the 1920s for Queen Soraya in conjunction with the construction of Darul Aman Palace for Amanullah Khan (see p. 21). Like that structure, Tajbeg Palace was heavily damaged during the fighting in the late 1980s and 1990s. Photo (2013) by Spc. Andrew Claire Baker, USA. *Department of Defense.*

Khan, later an influential mujahideen and governor of Herat, led a revolt of the 17th Infantry Division in Herat against the PDPA and Russian advisors based there. This revolt was unique in that power fell entirely into the hands of local insurgents.[27] According to press reports, mutineers went door to door hunting and executing Soviet advisors. Dissidents cut telephone communication, blocked the road from Kandahar to Herat, closed Shindand air base, and attacked Soviet citizens for ten days until armored Afghan military units arrived and Soviet MiGs carried out air strikes in Herat.[28]

Yuri V. Andropov, chairman of the KGB, told a crisis section of the Politburo on March 17, "Bearing in mind that we will be labeled as an aggressor, but in spite of that, under no circumstances can we lose Afghanistan."[29] The Soviets responded immediately with increased military aid: light tanks, armored personnel carriers, and Mi–24 Hinds, the most advanced Soviet helicopter gunship at the time.[30] In early April 1979, Gen. Alexei A. Yepishev, chief of the main political directorate of the Soviet army and navy, visited Kabul to evaluate the military and political situation and to express Soviet concerns to Prime Minister Taraki. Yepishev had experience putting down political unrest in Soviet satellites, having played a key role in the Soviet intervention in Czechoslovakia in 1968. After his visit, Soviet advisors made all major military decisions.[31] Soviet pilots routinely patrolled Afghan air space, and a Soviet division moved to the Afghan border.[32] In the summer of 1979, the Soviet air force took over Bagram and Shindand air bases. The Soviet Union also increased arms deliveries to Afghanistan, including T–62 tanks, MiG–21 and MiG–23 fighters, Su–20 bombers, Mi–24 helicopter gunships, and Mi–16 helicopter transports.[33] Despite increased arms shipments in the summer, the Politburo viewed intervention as less advisable, choosing to preserve détente and hoping for the best in Afghan stability.[34]

In August 1979, Gen. Ivan Pavlovskii, deputy minister of defense and commander in chief of Soviet ground forces, led a sixty-three-person Soviet military delegation, including eleven general officers, to evaluate the crisis in Afghanistan. When Pavlovskii returned to Moscow in November, he advised against military intervention. Consensus within the Politburo to invade was building, however. Taraki and Amin made at least sixteen formal requests for Soviet troops between mid-April and mid-December 1979, reinforcing the push in Moscow for intervention.[35] Three key Soviet officials in Kabul—the Soviet Ambassador to Afghanistan, Alexander

The remains of a Soviet aircraft (probably a MiG–21) at Bagram air base outside Kabul, February 2002, with U.S. Army UH–60 Black Hawk helicopters in the background. The Soviets took control of the air bases at Bagram and Shindand in the summer of 1979. *National Archives.*

As the war progressed, the Soviets built training facilities in Afghanistan, such as this one north of Kandahar. It later became a Taliban base. It is shown in a 2005 photo after U.S. forces captured the camp. Photo by PFC Leslie Angulo, USA. *Department of Defense/National Archives.*

M. Puzanov, chief of the KGB mission in Afghanistan; Lt. Gen. Boris Ivanov; and Lt. Gen. Lev N. Gorelov, the chief Soviet military advisor to Afghanistan—argued that "in view of possible stepped-up activity by the rebel formations in August and September . . . it is essential to respond affirmatively to the request from the Afghan friends and to send a special brigade to Kabul in the immediate future."[36]

The state of affairs rapidly disintegrated in September 1979 after Amin took control of the government from Taraki. Within the Soviet Politburo, leaders began to shift toward intervention, citing Amin's erratic behavior and the strategic importance of Afghanistan.[37] The KGB responded by launching Operation Zenith in October, dispersing special forces across Afghanistan to determine popular reaction to a Soviet intervention. In November and December, the Soviet military began to orchestrate it. A Soviet special forces battalion of Central Asian airborne troops deployed to Afghanistan on November 9. Soviet conventional ground forces moved to the Afghan border in late November.

On November 28, Lt. Gen. Viktor S. Paputin, first deputy minister of internal affairs, arrived in Kabul on a mission to pressure Amin to step down or to invite Soviet troops to assist in stabilizing Afghanistan. Amin refused, but the Soviet military continued with its plan. Two more Soviet battalions landed at Bagram air base north of Kabul in early December. On

December 12, the Politburo met and approved a handwritten resolution, "Concerning the Situation in A."[38] On December 18–19, Soviet troops cleared the highway to the Salang Pass.

By the end of 1979, the entire country was in revolt. Based on extensive firsthand contacts, Nake M. Kamrany described a broad-based Afghan movement against the Soviets: "It is not one person or one group that is resisting the Soviet system in Afghanistan. It is every Afghan in every village. And these villages do not have the means to communicate with each other. They have no system or means of communication." He continued: "What happens in Afghanistan is that each village has its own resistance in its own way. Some of them knock out a Soviet tank, some of them just wait and shoot at soldiers, some of them burn down a government building. In whatever form, it is a resistance from within."[39]

Louis Dupree observed four key struggles at the time:

- uncoordinated, generalized guerrilla war against the Kabul regime;
- competition, mainly in Peshawar, between conservative and moderate religious leaders in the Pashtun area to monopolize funds from friendly Arabs;
- attempts by mujahideen to establish local bases of power (Nuristan, Hazarajat, and Badakhshan) so that any new regime in Kabul would have to grant regional autonomy to the various ethnolinguistic groups; and
- the internal struggle for power within the Khalq leadership.[40]

U.S. National Security Advisor Zbigniew K. Brzezinski warned President Carter in March 1980 of Soviet "creeping intervention in Afghanistan."[41] More recent Russian analysis confirms the thesis that "mission creep" led to the Soviet invasion of Afghanistan.[42]

Officially, the Soviet invasion of Afghanistan began on December 24, 1979, when tens of thousands of ground troops crossed the Amu Darya into Afghanistan and 7,700 more flew to Bagram, Kabul, and Shindand air bases. The Soviet military brought exiled Parcham leaders, including Babrak Karmal, with them to install as the heads of a new pro-Moscow government. On December 27, a combined Soviet special forces group, with GRU, KGB, Ministry of Defense, and airborne elements, stormed Tajbeg Palace and killed Amin as part of Operation Storm 333.[43]

Less than two weeks after the incursion, President Carter declared that "the Soviet invasion of Afghanistan is the greatest threat to peace since the Second World War." Carter added a few weeks later that "the Soviets

Abandoned Soviet tanks in Bamyan Province. The Russians left a tremendous amount of materiél when they withdrew from Afghanistan in 1989, finding it impractical to transport it back across the Hindu Kush. Photo (2013) by Sgt. Christopher Bonebrake, USA. *Department of Defense.*

have seriously misjudged our own nation's strength and resolve and unity and determination and the condemnation that has accrued to them by the world community because of their invasion of Afghanistan."[44] The United States halted grain exports to the Soviet Union and led a boycott of the Summer Olympics in Moscow in 1980.[45] Brzezinski told the president that, with American help to Afghan forces, the Soviets might become ensnared in Afghanistan the way the United States had been in Vietnam.[46] The Reagan administration expanded this effort. In the early 1980s, Central Intelligence Agency (CIA) director William J. Casey developed a wide-ranging international coalition to fund and train the mujahideen movements.[47]

Karmal's new government proved unable to consolidate power with Soviet troops on the ground and, increasingly, the PDPA began shunning Soviet activities in Afghanistan.[48] The Soviet military did little to win goodwill, carrying out massive reprisals and forcing hundreds of thousands of Afghan refugees into Iran and Pakistan. For its part, the Afghan National Army suffered extensive desertions as troops left to join the mujahideen. The force, numbering 80,000 men at the beginning of 1979, declined to 50,000 in December 1979 and 25,000 at the end of 1980.[49] Extended age limits and service terms stabilized the force at 40,000 by 1986 despite the continued difficulties to conscript, organize, and mobilize troops. The Soviet Union brought a new generation of young Afghan "volunteers" to train, with ever more limited results.[50]

Strategically, the Soviet army focused on securing Kabul and the Afghan highway system linking Kabul to Kandahar, Herat, and Termez. Much of the countryside remained outside government control throughout the 1980s.[51] Soviet forces in Afghanistan operated under the command of the Fortieth Army headquarters in Kabul, with operational control and support in Termez. The original rules of engagement permitted Soviet soldiers only to return fire or to liberate captured Soviet advisors. After a major antigovernment and anti-Soviet demonstration in Kabul on February 21, 1980, Moscow ordered the Fortieth Army to "begin active operations together with the Afghan army to defeat the detachments of the armed opposition."[52] Soviet troops were unprepared for local Afghan resistance and the resilient guerrilla force.[53]

From 1979 until 1989, the Fortieth Army conducted 220 operations and 400 combined operations. Increasingly frustrated with the lack of long-term success against an elusive insurgent enemy, the Soviets turned to using aerial "butterfly" mines, chemical weapons, and even booby-trapped toys.[54] Afghan forces were under Soviet operational control throughout the war.[55]

President James E. Carter Jr. and his national security advisor, Zbigniew K. Brzezinski. Carter called the Soviet invasion of Afghanistan the "greatest threat to peace since the Second World War." Brzezinski speculated that the Soviets might become ensnared in Afghanistan the way the U.S. had been in Vietnam. *National Archives.*

President Ronald W. Reagan with Soviet leader Mikhail S. Gorbachev at a summit in Reykjavik, Iceland, in October 1986. Gorbachev ultimately made the decision for the Soviets to withdraw from Afghanistan, beginning in 1988. *Reagan Presidential Library.*

The conflict resulted in inestimable damage to Afghanistan's already poor infrastructure and economy. By January 1980, growing unrest had driven more than 400,000 Afghan refugees to Pakistan and more than 30,000 to Iran.[56] On "Afghanistan Day," March 21, 1982, President Reagan implored:

> The tragedy in Afghanistan must not be allowed to drag on endlessly. This conflict imperils the stability of the region. It has seriously poisoned the international environment. Afghanistan itself is being brutalized. The suffering of the Afghan people is immense. I earnestly hope that the Soviet Union will join with us in an urgent effort to bring a swift withdrawal of its forces to end this needless conflict.[57]

Two years later, Vice President George H. W. Bush visited a refugee camp in Peshawar, Pakistan, and told his audience: "My dear Afghan brethren, you and your people have suffered greatly. You have shown courage and fortitude beyond the usual measure. You have my heartfelt admiration and that of my countrymen. You have earned the admiration of free men everywhere."[58] At the same time, U.S. leaders made a concerted effort to thank Pakistan for its support of Afghanistan and Afghan refugees.[59]

Soviet military leaders had advocated withdrawal once Karmal's new government was in place in 1980.[60] When the Afghan army proved unable to provide the necessary security, however, Soviet political leaders wavered and did not make a decision. In general, Soviet leaders lacked commitment to resolve the crisis in Afghanistan as they dealt with a host of domestic issues from 1981 to 1985. Not until Mikhail S. Gorbachev came to power, and following a yearlong attempt at a military solution, did the Soviets advocate the National Reconciliation Campaign and put a new Afghan leader in place to facilitate a Soviet departure.[61] On May 5, 1986, Karmal resigned and Dr. Mohammad Najibullah, head of the paramilitary Government Intelligence Service (Khadamat-e Etela'at-e Dawlati, or KHAD), succeeded him. The Soviets gave him two years to prepare for their military withdrawal. When the Soviet minister of foreign affairs, Eduard A. Shevardnadze, and long-time Soviet ambassador to the United States Anatoly F. Dobrynin visited Kabul in December 1986 to evaluate the political situation, they observed, "Of friendly feeling toward the Soviet people, which had existed in Afghanistan for decades, little remains. Many people have died, and not all of them were bandits. . . . The state apparatus is functioning poorly. Our advice and help is ineffective. . . . Everything that we have done and are doing is incompatible with the moral character of our country."[62]

In some instances, the U.S. Air Force flew Afghan rebels to the United States or Europe for treatment, such as these arriving at Norton Air Force Bace, California, in 1986. They were transported by a 375th Aeromedical Airlift Wing C–9A Nightingale. At left is Col. Marvin Ervina, commander of the 63d Military Airlift Wing. *Department of Defense.*

The United States continued to express support for the anti-Soviet Afghans. President Reagan told Afghan resistance leader Burhanuddin Rabbani during a White House visit in June 1986 that "in your struggle to regain your nation's independence, the American people stand with you. This policy has broad and deep bipartisan support; it is an unshakeable commitment. Your goal is our goal—the freedom of Afghanistan. We will not let you down."[63]

One of the signature details of the U.S. campaign to undermine the Soviet occupation of Afghanistan was the CIA effort to supply Stinger missiles to the mujahideen.[64] "Charlie Wilson's War," as it came to be known, was a riveting yarn with covert intrigue, but it had little impact on the war itself. Rodric Braithwaite observed that "Gorbachev took the decision to withdraw from Afghanistan a full year before the first Stinger was fired."[65] There is little doubt that the Stinger missile affected tactics—night flying, combat landings, high-altitude bombing, and the deployment of flares—but it did not undermine Soviet air power. "While the Stinger, first introduced in combat in September 1986, did give the mujahideen an important antiaircraft tool," Kalinovsky explained, "it hardly changed the course of the war."[66]

On May 15, 1988, Soviet troops began to withdraw, and the commander of the Fortieth Army, Gen. Boris V. Gromov, crossed the Friendship Bridge into the Soviet Union on February 15, 1989, as the last Soviet combatant to leave Afghanistan.[67] On the pullout, Soviet journalist Alexander Prokhanov wrote, "The departure of our troops is not a defeat. The army is in excellent fighting form. The morale of officers and men is high. It is an organized departure from a country that we did not intend to occupy, did not intend to destroy and subjugate. The troops are leaving as the vector of politics changes into reverse, and the army follows that vector."[68] After the Soviet withdrawal, the Afghan government maintained a weekly 600-truck convoy to the Soviet Union, and the Soviet air force continued to airlift supplies.[69]

Despite their enthusiasm for the success of the mujahideen resistance, many U.S. officials held reservations about its viability as a political movement. In 1988, Robert B. Oakley, the U.S. ambassador to Pakistan, observed that "the fight against 'heroin-Kalashnikov culture' is almost as critical to the future of Pakistan's security as the fight against Soviet domination of Afghanistan has been."[70] It remains an open question why U.S. officials invested so little in the so-called moderate mujahideen, particularly groups led by Pir Ahmed Gailani and Pir Sibghatullah Mojaddedi.

Instead, U.S. policy makers focused on ousting the Najibullah government. Assistant Secretary of State for Near Eastern and South Asian

U.S. Congressman Charles N. "Charlie" Wilson (D-TX), who worked with CIA operatives to have Stinger missles provided to the Afghan resistance, is shown in a personal photo with mujahideen fighters in Afghanistan. *Naval History and Heritage Command Photo Archive.*

Affairs John H. Kelly released a statement in March 1990: "We believe that no stable political settlement is achievable as long as the Najibullah regime remains in power. The Resistance is both united and passionate on this point: a transfer of power away from the present regime and to a new government is necessary for this chapter, with all its attendant tragedy, to be brought to a close."[71] In September 1991, U.S. secretary of state James A. Baker III and Soviet foreign minister Boris N. Pankin released a joint statement agreeing on the cessation of hostilities, support for elections during the transition period, the repatriation of refugees, and the prompt reconstruction of Afghanistan. Both parties pledged to cut off arms supplies by January 1, 1992.[72]

When the Soviet Union formally dissolved in December 1991, however, its military support to Afghanistan vanished. Najibullah's government lasted until April 27, 1992, when mujahideen forces entered Kabul and a new civil war commenced.[73] As Thomas J. Barfield explained, "In retrospect, it was clear that the resistance had been given a task they were incapable of accomplishing. The mujahideen had no previous experience in assaulting heavily defended cities, and their forces had never been integrated into a common defense structure."[74]

As the 1990s progressed, Russia proved disinterested in playing an influential role in Kabul.[75] Meanwhile, U.S. relations with Pakistan, its Afghan partner, frayed as Pakistan sought nuclear armament. Conflict in Afghanistan shifted from guerrilla warfare supported by international actors to more conventional and territorialized war.[76]

From the Soviet
Withdrawal to 9/11

In his study of the Soviet withdrawal, historian Artemy M. Kalinovsky argued that Mohammad Najibullah "found ways to sabotage Soviet-led outreach when he felt it suited his interests. After the Soviets withdrew, the PDPA took more courageous steps in terms of opening up the government and society, establishing links with tribal leaders, and shedding its communist image."[1] Still, challenges existed that continued to undermine the already weak Afghan government. Corruption pilfered 85 to 90 percent of Soviet aid at the end of the 1980s.[2] Even more ominously, well-funded, Pakistani-supported military-political organizations were waiting for the collapse of the PDPA to establish their own government in Afghanistan.

On March 18, 1992, mujahideen forces led by Abdul Rashid Dostum, with support from Ahmad Shah Massoud, an influential Tajik mujahideen leader, captured Mazar-i Sharif without resistance. By April 14, Massoud occupied Charikar, Jabal ul-Seraj, and Bagram air base. Najibullah unsuccessfully attempted to flee to India but instead took refuge at the United Nations offices in Kabul.[3]

While several military factions descended on the capital, mujahideen party leaders met in Peshawar, Pakistan, to devise a political solution. The Peshawar Accords, a peace and power-sharing agreement among the major Afghan mujahideen parties, created the new Islamic Republic of Afghanistan and established an interim government, under the leadership of Sibghatullah Mojaddedi, to be followed by general elections.[4] Mojaddedi became president on April 28; Pakistan, the European Economic Community, and the United States recognized the new state on the same day. On April 29, Massoud entered Kabul with his army.[5] Gulbuddin Hekmatyar's Islamic Party (Hizb-e Islami), however, refused to participate and continued its assault on Kabul.

In early May, Dostum, Hekmetyar, and Massoud began to articulate their competition for Kabul. Mojaddedi requested an extension to his power-sharing agreement but was refused by the other mujahideen leaders. On June 29, Mojaddedi stepped down and handed power to Burhanuddin

Rabbani, leader of the Islamic Society of Afghanistan (Jamiat-e Islami). Rabbani chose Massoud as his minister of defense. For the next two years, Massoud's forces waged continuous warfare against Hekmatyar and his allies, and the conflict regionalized within Afghanistan. Kabul remained the epicenter of war throughout this period.[6]

Since the early 1980s, Pakistan's Inter-Services Intelligence (ISI) had supported Afghan parties that shared President Zia ul-Haq's view of Islamizing Pakistani society.[7] With the failure of Pakistan's primary ally, Hekmatyar, to capture Kabul, Pakistani intelligence and military leaders invested in a new militant political group of young Afghan refugees and veterans of the anti-Soviet jihad, the Taliban. It had initially focused on gaining influence in the area around Kandahar and securing transportation networks for legal and illegal commerce, but the Taliban soon began a campaign to occupy other parts of Afghanistan. Martin K. Ewans described the group's impressive arrival to the civil war: "The Taliban forces that proceeded to advance through Afghanistan in the winter of 1994–1995 were equipped with tanks, APCs, artillery, and even aircraft."[8]

Pakistan's official supporters were not the only advocates for the Taliban. As journalist Gretchen Peters explained, "Mullah Omar's movement—almost from its inception—was highly dependent on and intertwined with the opium network spanning the Pakistan-Afghanistan border. Drug traffickers and tribes growing poppy were critical to the Taliban's swift and astonishing rise to power." According to Peters, "Fueled by drug money and joined at the hip with al-Qaeda, the Taliban turned Afghanistan into the world's first fully fledged narco-terror state."[9]

The Taliban succeeded in providing security to the Afghan people where other mujahideen movements failed. Mullah Muhammad Omar led the initial Taliban group in southern Kandahar Province as a response to local banditry, brutality by local militias, and broad social malaise.[10] While the two major mujahideen groups, Hizb-e-Islami and Jamiat-e Islami, had an antagonistic relationship with young Talibs, Omar was associated with the moderate group, Islamic Revolution Movement (Harakat-e Inqilab-e Islami) that was part of the Peshawar Seven, supported by the United States and Pakistan.[11] That moderation proved to be an illusion. Anthropologist Olivier Roy argued in 1998 that "the problem with the Taliban is that they mean what they say. . . . The Taliban are not a factor for stabilization in Afghanistan."[12] Conversely, Kalinovsky observed, "The Taliban earned Pakistan's support because they held the promise of restoring order and of being useful to the ISI. Similarly, the United States largely turned a blind eye to the Taliban and their excesses."[13] This stabilization was a mirage.

An opium poppy field in the Marja district of Helmand Province. The Taliban, almost from its inception, was dependent on the drug trade and built a strong network in this region. Photo (2012) by Sgt. Michael P. Snody, USMC. *Department of Defense.*

Direct Russian support for the Afghan government ended with the rise of the Taliban in 1994. After this point, the Russian government engaged in complex proxy battles in a new phase of the Afghan civil war alongside other regional powers, including Pakistan, India, Iran, Saudi Arabia, and Uzbekistan. Faced with the prospect of Islamic revolution in Central Asia, the Russian government began to support militias with anti-Soviet pasts. In 1996, Massoud and Dostum, two former rivals, joined to resist the growing Taliban threat and formed the United Islamic Front, also known as the Northern Alliance. Massoud had played a major role in the resistance against the Soviet Union during the 1980s, earning him the distinctions the "Lion of Panjshir" and the "Afghan who won the Cold War." Dostum, considered the leader of Afghanistan's Uzbek community, had fought on the Soviet side until the collapse of Najibullah's government in 1992 and shifted alliances on several occasions thereafter. This pair and their forces proved little match for the well-equipped Taliban.[14]

In May 1996, Osama bin Laden, under pressure from the Saudi, Libyan, and Egyptian governments, shifted the base of al-Qaeda operations from Sudan to Afghanistan. Bin Laden thus returned to his jihadist roots, where his leadership during the battles of Jaji was lauded by Arab journalists and served as his introduction to the power of the press.[15] As Peter L. Bergen observed, "The Afghan war changed bin Laden. The humble, young,

Northern Alliance troops, who fought with U.S. forces against the Taliban in the early stages of Operation Enduring Freedom, at Bagram air base to greet U.S. secretary of defense Donald H. Rumsfeld, December 16, 2001. Photo by Jim Garamone. *Department of Defense.*

monosyllabic millionaire with the open checkbook who had first visited Pakistan in the early 1980s would, by the middle of the decade, launch an ambitious plan to confront the Soviets directly inside Afghanistan with a group of Arabs under his command. That cadre of Arabs would provide the nucleus of al-Qaeda."[16] While the Saudis had cut off his wealth in Sudan, bin Laden benefitted from his return to Afghanistan, forging a mutually advantageous relationship that drew upon Arab financial contributions to the Taliban in the Afghan civil war and buttressed the Taliban's international reputation.[17]

From Afghanistan, bin Laden declared war against the United States in August 1996, citing the continuing presence of U.S. forces in Saudi Arabia five years after the Persian Gulf War and declaring that "the walls of oppression and humiliation cannot be demolished except in a rain of bullets."[18] Despite multiple international efforts to dislodge him from Afghanistan, bin Laden and the Taliban remained codependent: bin Laden supported the Taliban's military and political efforts to consolidate Afghanistan as an "Islamic state," while the Taliban provided protection for bin Laden.[19] Ultimately, bin Laden's public vitriol clashed with Mullah Omar's political interests, and the latter "invited" bin Laden to Kandahar in 1997.[20]

The Taliban had brought much of northern Afghanistan under its rule by 1998, buying off rivals, carrying out systematic attacks on civilians, and forcing Dostum into exile in Turkey. Only Massoud proved able to defend his territory in northeastern Afghanistan from Taliban militias, but that success ended with his assassination, at the hands of al-Qaeda members posing as journalists, on September 9, 2001.[21] Two days later, al-Qaeda

A propaganda poster, found by U.S. troops in 2002, showing al-Qaeda leader Osama bin Laden. The architect of the 9/11 attacks was killed in Pakistan in 2011 by U.S. Special Forces. *National Archives.*

terrorists launched an assault on the United States that led to direct U.S. military engagement in Afghanistan.

After weeks of unsuccessful negotiations with the Taliban to turn over al-Qaeda militants involved in terrorism in the United States, U.S.-led coalition forces initiated a campaign on October 7, 2001, to establish air superiority, destroy terrorist training camps, kill or capture al-Qaeda leaders, and eliminate terrorist activities in Afghanistan. As U.S. forces joined with the Northern Alliance and began to capture cities across Afghanistan in November and December, U.S. officials observed a complex system of strategic interests, challenges, and realities on the ground.

A U.S. Air Force F–15E Strike Eagle from the 332d Air Expeditionary Group takes off for a mission over Afghanistan during the early stages of Operation Enduring Freedom, November 7, 2001. *National Archives.*

*　　*　　*

Reaching back to the history of the Soviet war in Afghanistan, Kalinovsky made an intriguing comparison, writing in 2011 that "Hamid Karzai, who took power after U.S. forces helped to topple the Taliban in 2001, now seems cast in the role of Babrak Karmal—distrusted by his patrons and by his countrymen, isolated and with little influence even over his supporters."[22] As U.S. forces continue their own withdrawal from Afghanistan, the lessons of the Soviet experience weigh heavily. Yet a longer view of the U.S. engagement in Afghanistan reveals a more nuanced and patient approach. The United States has long supported Afghanistan with economic aid and diplomatic friendship in measured terms and hopeful enthusiasm. This pattern will surely persist in the twenty-first century.

It is best to remember Winston S. Churchill's poignant observation about the Afghans: "They, when they fight among themselves, bear little malice, and the combatants not infrequently make friends over the corpses of their comrades or suspend operations for a festival or horse race. At the end of the contest cordial relations are at once re-established. And yet so full of contractions is their character."[23]

Notes

INTRODUCTION

1. Giving the 1907 Romanes Lecture, Lord Curzon had just returned from the position as viceroy of India (1899–1905). He was very familiar with Afghanistan, and he had traveled extensively in Central and South Asia in the 1880s and 1890s. He had served as under-secretary of state for India (1891–92) and under-secretary of state for foreign affairs (1895–98). Lord Curzon of Kedleston, *Frontiers* (Westport, CT: Greenwood Press, 1976), 7, quoted in Seth G. Jones, *In the Graveyard of Empires: America's War in Afghanistan* (New York: Norton, 2009), 277.

2. For Afghanistan's ethnic groups, see Thomas J. Barfield, *Afghanistan: A Cultural and Political History* (Princeton, NJ: Princeton University Press, 2010), 66–67; Robert Nichols, *A History of Pashtun Migration, 1775–2006* (New York: Oxford University Press, 2008), 24–63; Vartan Gregorian, *The Emergence of Modern Afghanistan: Politics of Reform and Modernization, 1880–1946* (Stanford, CA: Stanford University Press, 1969), 46–51; Amin Saikal, *Modern Afghanistan: A History of Struggle and Survival* (New York: Palgrave Macmillan, 2004), 20–21; Larry P. Goodson, *Afghanistan's Endless War: State Failure, Regional Politics, and the Rise of the Taliban* (Seattle: University of Washington Press, 2001), 29–30; Louis Dupree, *Afghanistan* (1973; reprint, Oxford: Oxford University Press, 1997), 57–65.

3. Although "Pashtun" is now conventional, historical references use a variety of terms for this same ethnic group, depending on the geographic location of the sources. The British used "Pathan," drawing from the Hindi term. Kandahari and southern Afghans used "Pashtun" and "Pushtun." Northern Afghans, including Tajiks and Uzbeks, as well as groups in the Trans-Khyber region, used "Pakhtun" or "Pukhtun." For this group, see Brian Glyn Williams, *Afghanistan Declassified: A Guide to America's Longest War* (Philadelphia: University of Pennsylvania Press, 2012), 16–27; Barnett R. Rubin, *The Fragmentation of Afghanistan: State Formation and Collapse in the International System*, 2d ed. (New Haven, CT: Yale University Press, 2002), 26–29; Olaf K. Caroe, *The Pathans: 550 B.C.–A.D. 1957* (New York: St. Martin's, 1958); Akbar S. Ahmed, *Pukhtun Economy and Society: Traditional Structure and Economic Development in a Tribal Society* (London: Routledge & Kegan Paul, 1980); Colin M. Enriquez, *The Pathan Borderland: A Consecutive Account of the Country and People on and beyond the Indian Frontier from Chitral to Dera Ismail Khan*, 2d ed. (Calcutta, India: Thacker, Spink, and Co., 1921); Rob Hager, "State, Tribe, and Empire in Afghan Inter-Polity Relations," in Richard Tapper, ed., *The Conflict of Tribe and State in Iran and Afghanistan* (New York: St. Martin's, 1983), 83–118.

4. Goodson, *Afghanistan's Endless War*, 25. As Winston S. Churchill put it: "The people of one valley fight with those of the next. To the quarrels of communities are added the combats of individuals. Khan assails khan, each supported by his retainers. Every tribesman

has a blood feud with his neighbor. Every man's hand is against the other, and all against the stranger." Churchill, *The Story of the Malakand Field Force* (1898; reprint, Mineola, NY: Dover Publications, 2010), 3. According to a proverb, Pashtuns fight for three reasons: "zar, zan, zamin" (gold, women, and land).

5. Barfield, *Afghanistan*, 19; Gregorian, *Emergence of Modern Afghanistan*, 25–51; Dupree, *Afghanistan*, 57–65; Saikal, *Modern Afghanistan*, 20–21. For a color rendition of the map on p. 3, see http://www.loc.gov/item/92684507.

ONE

1. Charles Miller, *Khyber, British India's North West Frontier: The Story of an Imperial Migraine* (New York: Macmillan, 1977), xiv, 11–12.

2. Abdul Hai Habibi, "Paxto Literature at a Glance," *Afghanistan* 20, no. 4 (1968): 60, quoted in Louis Dupree, *Afghanistan* (1973; reprint, Oxford: Oxford University Press, 1997), 337.

3. Thomas J. Barfield, *Afghanistan: A Cultural and Political History* (Princeton, NJ: Princeton University Press, 2010), 99.

4. Dupree, *Afghanistan*, 338; Amin Saikal, *Modern Afghanistan: A History of Struggle and Survival* (New York: Palgrave Macmillan, 2004), 28. The Sikh Empire (1799–1849) forged a powerful state in northern India until it was conquered by British forces in the mid-nineteenth century.

5. Dupree, *Afghanistan*, 334; Saikal, *Modern Afghanistan*, 24–27.

6. Barfield, *Afghanistan*, 48; Vartan Gregorian, *The Emergence of Modern Afghanistan: Politics of Reform and Modernization, 1880–1946* (Stanford, CA: Stanford University Press, 1969), 98, 104; Saikal, *Modern Afghanistan*, 33–34; Martin Ewans, *Afghanistan: A Short History of Its People and Politics* (New York: Perennial, 2002), 37.

7. Malcolm E. Yapp, *Strategies of British India: Britain, Iran, and Afghanistan, 1798–1850* (Oxford: Clarendon Press, 1980), 238–39.

8. Capt. Arthur Conolly of the 6th Bengal Light Cavalry, a British intelligence officer, coined the term "Great Game" around 1831 to explain the competition between Russia and Britain in Asia. Conolly published a two-volume work, *Journey to the North of India, Overland from England, through Russia, Persia and Affghaunistaun*, in 1834 and was beheaded in 1842 in Bukhara (in current-day Uzbekistan) on the order of the Afghan amir. Rudyard Kipling widely popularized the term "Great Game" in his 1901 novel *Kim*. Peter Hopkirk, *The Great Game: The Struggle for Empire in Central Asia* (New York: Kodansha America, 1994), 1–2, 123; Saikal, *Modern Afghanistan*, 287 n. 43.

9. Karl E. Meyer and Shareen Blair Brysac, *Tournament of Shadows: The Great Game and the Race for Empire in Central Asia* (Washington, DC: Counterpoint, 1999), 156.

10. Joseph J. Collins, *Understanding War in Afghanistan* (Washington, DC: National Defense University Press, 2011), 17.

11. Sir Percy M. Sykes, *A History of Afghanistan*, 2 vols. (London: Macmillan, 1940), 1:401–2; Gregorian, *Emergence of Modern Afghanistan*, 75.

12. John William Kaye, *History of the War in Afghanistan*, 2 vols. (London: R. Bentley, 1851), 1:130.

13. Ben Macintyre, *The Man Who Would Be King: The First American in Afghanistan* (New York: Farrar, Straus and Giroux, 2004). See also Josiah Harlan, *Central Asia: Personal Narrative of General Josiah Harlan, 1823–1841*, ed. Frank E. Ross (London: Luzac, 1939); Josiah Harlan, *A Memoir of India and Avghanistan* (Philadelphia: J. Dobson, 1842).

14. Gregorian, *Emergence of Modern Afghanistan*, 139.

15. Barnett R. Rubin, *The Fragmentation of Afghanistan: State Formation and Collapse in the International System*, 2d ed. (New Haven, CT: Yale University Press, 2002), 48.

16. Dupree, *Afghanistan*, 418–19.

17. 'Abd al-Rahman Khan, *The Life of Abdur Rahman, Amir of Afghanistan*, 2 vols. (London: J. Murray, 1900), 2:176–77.

18. Barfield, *Afghanistan*, 5. Also see the survey of Abdur Rahman's reign in Saikal, *Modern Afghanistan*, 37–41.

19. Saikal, *Modern* Afghanistan, 40–41; Nancy Tapper, "Abd Al-Rahman's North-West Frontier: The Pashtun Colonisation of Afghan Turkistan," in Richard Tapper, ed., *The Conflict of Tribe and State in Iran and Afghanistan* (New York: St. Martin's, 1983), 253 (quote). Abdur Rahman also embraced the title "light of the nation and religion" (*zia-ul-millat-wa-ud din*) to reflect his broad, interethnic dominance.

20. Tapper, "Al-Rahman's North-West Frontier," 233–61.

21. Abdur Rahman did, however, abolish the *samardeh*, a tax on non-Pashtuns.

22. Barfield, *Afghanistan*, 155; Rubin, *Fragmentation of Afghanistan*, 90.

23. Gregorian, *Emergence of Modern Afghanistan*, 134.

24. Barfield, *Afghanistan*, 161.

25. al-Rahman Khan, *Life of Abdur Rahman*, 2:280. Also see Dupree, *Afghanistan*, 415.

26. al-Rahman Khan, *Life of Abdur Rahman*, 2:78.

27. Richard F. Nyrop and Donald M. Seekins, eds., *Afghanistan: A Country Study*, 5th ed. (Washington, DC: Library of Congress, 1986), 38, http://lcweb2.loc.gov/frd/cs/aftoc.html. For the major sections of the agreement, see Ludwig W. Adamec, *Historical Dictionary of Afghanistan*, 3d ed. (Lanham, MD: Scarecrow Press, 2003), 399–402.

28. Saikal, *Modern Afghanistan*, 39.

29. al-Rahman Khan, *Life of Abdur Rahman*, 2:158, 164.

30. An excellent historical study on the early stages of the frontier debate is Yapp, *Strategies of British India.*

31. al-Rahman Khan, *Life of Abdur Rahman*, 2:174.

32. Ibid., 2:171–72.

33. Ibid., 2:158, 178.

34. Rüdiger Schöch, "Afghan Refugees in Pakistan during the 1980s: Cold War Politics and Registration Practice" (Research Paper No. 157, United Nations High Commission for Refugees, Geneva, Switzerland, June 2008), http://www.unhcr.org/4868daad2.html.

Two

1. Clifford Orwin, "Stasis and Plague: Thucydides on the Dissolution of Society," *Journal of Politics* 4 (November 1988): 834; Thucydides, *The Peloponnesian War* (3.82); Thucydides, *The Peloponnesian War*, trans. Thomas Hobbes (Chicago: University of Chicago Press, 1989), 204.

2. Barnett R. Rubin, *The Fragmentation of Afghanistan: State Formation and Collapse in the International System*, 2d ed. (New Haven, CT: Yale University Press, 2002), 52.

3. Vartan Gregorian, *The Emergence of Modern Afghanistan: Politics of Reform and Modernization, 1880–1946* (Stanford, CA: Stanford University Press, 1969), 393–94. For an overview of Habibullah's reign, see Amin Saikal, *Modern Afghanistan: A History of Struggle and Survival* (New York: Palgrave Macmillan, 2004), 42–59.

4. Gregorian, *Emergence of Modern Afghanistan*, 164; Saikal, *Modern Afghanistan*, 45–46.

5. Gregorian, *Emergence of Modern Afghanistan*, 166.

6. Ibid., 206. For British attempts to undermine Habibullah, see Saikal, *Modern Afghanistan*, 53–55.

7. Gregorian, *Emergence of Modern Afghanistan*, 184. Mahmud Sami, a Turkish colonel, ran the college after 1907.

8. Leon B. Poullada and Leila D. J. Poullada, *The Kingdom of Afghanistan and the United States: 1828–1973* (Lincoln, NE: Center for Afghan Studies, University of Nebraska at Omaha, and Dageforde Publishing, 1995), 13. See also A. C. Jewett and Marjorie Jewett Bell, *An American Engineer in Afghanistan: From the Letters and Notes of A. C. Jewett* (Minneapolis: University of Minnesota Press, 1948). Various Afghans informed Jewett that he was the first American to visit their country in decades. One told him that the last American had been there in 1840; another said 1880. The Poulladas piece together stories of this and other early Afghan-American contact up through the 1930s in the first two chapters of their book.

9. "Convention between Great Britain and Russia Concerning the Interests of Their States on the Continent of Asia," September 24, 1907, *Papers Relating to the Foreign Relations of the United States, 1907* (Washington, DC: U.S. Department of State, 1910), 1:552, http://digicoll. library.wisc.edu/cgi-bin/FRUS/FRUS-idx?type=turn&id=FRUS.FRUS1907v01&entity=FRUS. FRUS1907v01.p0664&q1=552.

10. Gregorian, *Emergence of Modern Afghanistan*, 211–12; Saikal, *Modern Afghanistan*, 51–56.

11. For the Turkish-German mission to Habibullah, see Gregorian, *Emergence of Modern Afghanistan*, 220–23; for the entire period of the war, see Ludwig W. Adamec, *Afghanistan's Foreign Affairs to the Mid-Twentieth Century: Relations with the USSR, Germany, and Britain* (Tucson: University of Arizona Press, 1974), 15–41.

12. Gregorian, *Emergence of Modern Afghanistan*, 227–31; Louis Dupree, *Afghanistan* (1973; reprint, Oxford: Oxford University Press, 1997), 442–43; Martin Ewans, *Afghanistan: A Short History of Its People and Politics* (New York: Perennial, 2002), 120–26; Thomas J. Barfield, *Afghanistan: A Cultural and Political History* (Princeton, NJ: Princeton University Press, 2010), 181–83; Adamec, *Afghanistan's Foreign Affairs*, 46–51; Saikal, *Modern Afghanistan*, 63–65.

13. Gregorian, *Emergence of Modern Afghanistan*, 230; Ewans, *Afghanistan*, 122–23.

14. Saikal, *Modern Afghanistan*, 62–63.

15. According to Saikal, the wording of the treaty "was so ambiguous as to allow the Afghans to read in it British acknowledgement of their full independence; and the British to find grounds in it still to make 'sphere of influence' claims on the country." Ibid., 64. See also Adamec, *Afghanistan's Foreign Affairs*, 90–98; Sir Percy M. Sykes, *A History of Afghanistan*, 2 vols. (London: Macmillan, 1940), 2:284, 358–59.

16. Ewans, *Afghanistan*, 124–25.

17. Adamec, *Afghanistan's Foreign Affairs*, 52–57.

18. Leonid B. Teplinskii, *Sovetsko-Afganskie otnosheniia* [Soviet-Afghan Relations], *1919–1960* (Moscow: Izd-vo sotsial'no-ekon. lit-ry, 1961); Sergei B. Panin, *Sovetskaia Rossiia i Afganistan* [Soviet Russia and Afghanistan], *1919–1929* (Irkutsk: Irkutsk State Pedagogical University, 1998); Mikhail Volodarskii, *Sovety i ikh iuzhnye sosedi, Iran i Afganistan* [The Soviets and Their Southern Neighbors, Iran and Afghanistan] *(1917–1933)* (London: Overseas Publications, 1985).

19. Panin, *Sovetskaia Rossiia i Afganistan*, 44; Adamec, *Afghanistan's Foreign Affairs*, 56–57.

20. For the Jadid movement in Central Asia, see Adeeb Khalid, *The Politics of Muslim Cultural Reform: Jadidism in Central Asia* (Berkeley: University of California Press, 1998); Alexandre Bennigsen, "The Soviet Union and Muslim Guerrilla Wars, 1920–1981: Lessons for Afghanistan" (Rand Note N–1707/1, Rand Corporation, Santa Monica, CA, August 1981), http://www.rand.org/content/dam/rand/pubs/notes/2005/N1707.1.pdf.

21. Volodarskii, *Iran i Afganistan*, 178. See also Adamec, *Afghanistan's Foreign Affairs*, 70–71, on Enver Pasha's leadership of the "Old Bukhara" forces at Termez, Baisun, and Shahr-i Sabz.

22. Adamec, *Afghanistan's Foreign Affairs*, 69–72; Saikal, *Modern Afghanistan*, 68–74; Gregorian, *Emergence of Modern Afghanistan*, 234–39. Saikal observed that "Amanullah's inability to provide active support for the Central Asian Muslims, in particular the Basmachi Movement, markedly undermined his credibility. From the start, one of his main pillars of legitimacy was a claim to be, above everything else, an Islamic ruler; but when a real test came to substantiate this claim in the face of Soviet actions, he could not do so" (p. 74).

23. Ludwig W. Adamec, "Afghan Air Force," in Adamec, *Historical Dictionary of Afghanistan*, 4th ed. (Lanham, MD: Scarecrow Press, 2012), 38. Also see British intelligence reports on the early Afghan air force in Anita L. P. Burdett, ed., *Afghanistan Strategic Intelligence: British Records, 1919–1970*, 4 vols. (London: Archive Editions, 2002), 2:125–37.

24. Gregorian, *Emergence of Modern Afghanistan*, 255.

25. Maurice Pernot, *L'Inquiétude de l'Orient: En Asie Musulmane* (Paris: Hachette, 1927), 43; Adamec, *Afghanistan's Foreign Affairs*, 108; Gregorian, *Emergence of Modern Afghanistan*, 247.

26. Saikal, *Modern Afghanistan*, 73–79; Gregorian, *Emergence of Modern Afghanistan*, 239–54.

27. Saikal, *Modern Afghanistan*, 82–88; Gregorian, *Emergence of Modern Afghanistan*, 254–56.

28. See Leon B. Poullada, *Reform and Rebellion in Afghanistan, 1919–1929: King Amanullah's Failure to Modernize a Tribal Society* (Ithaca, NY: Cornell University Press, 1973), 143–95, for a comprehensive study of Amanullah's reforms and the rise of tribal power.

29. Senzil K. Nawid, *Religious Response to Social Change in Afghanistan, 1919–29: King Aman-Allah and the Afghan Ulama* (Costa Mesa, CA: Mazda Publishers, 1999), 138.

30. Gregorian, *Emergence of Modern Afghanistan*, 266, 278–79; Grigorii S. Agabekov, *O.G.P.U.: The Russian Secret Terror* (New York: Brentano's, 1931), 159–60; Grigorii S. Agabekov, *Ch. K. za rabotoi* (Berlin: Strela, 1931), 276–83; Joseph Castagné, "Soviet Imperialism in Afghanistan," *Foreign Affairs* 13 (July 1935): 698–703.

31. Gregorian, *Emergence of Modern Afghanistan*, 280–81.

32. The title "amir" connoted a commander, general, admiral, or prince, while "malik" signified a king or chief.

33. Saikal, *Modern Afghanistan*, 99; Poullada, *Reform and Rebellion in Afghanistan*, 116–18, 194–95. Shah Mahmud Khan and Shah Wali Khan, along with Mohammad Hashim Khan, would play influential roles later as the uncles of both Mohammad Zahir Shah and Mohammad Daud.

34. Adamec, *Afghanistan's Foreign Affairs*, 202–4; Gregorian, *Emergence of Modern Afghanistan*, 321–32.

35. Hazaras are Persian-speaking Shia Muslims in central Afghanistan; Mangals are a Pashtun tribe in Paktia and Khost; and Mohmands are Pashtuns in Kunduz, Nangarhar, and Kunar. Gregorian, *Emergence of Modern Afghanistan*, 297.

36. Ibid., 297–98.

37. Abdul Khaliq was immediately apprehended and publicly executed. His relatives, fellow students, and teachers were executed as well. In Pashtun tribal code, *badal* (revenge) requires retribution for insults or the shedding of blood. The practice serves as a deterrent to lawlessness but often results in destructive cycles of violence. See Adamec, *Historical Dictionary*, 10, 71.

38. Saikal, *Modern Afghanistan*, 106–8; Gregorian, *Emergence of Modern Afghanistan*, 375–78.

39. Adamec, *Afghanistan's Foreign Affairs*, 213–27.

40. Ibid., 216–17; Gregorian, *Emergence of Modern Afghanistan*, 378–92.

41. Saikal, *Modern Afghanistan*, 109–10.

42. Ernest F. Fox, *Travels in Afghanistan, 1937–1938* (New York: Macmillan, 1943), xvii.

43. *Department of State Treaty Information*, Bulletin No. 95, August 1937, 5, 33–35; Gregorian, *Emergence of Modern Afghanistan*, 376–78; Adamec, *Afghanistan's Foreign Affairs*, 233–34.

44. Saikal, *Modern Afghanistan*, 110, 113–15.

45. *American Foreign Policy: Basic Documents, 1977–1980* (Washington, DC: Department of State, 1983), 883.

46. Milan L. Hauner, "The Soviet Threat to Afghanistan and India, 1938–1940," *Modern Asian Studies* 15 (April 1981): 287–309. For a survey of Afghanistan's balancing act with Germany, Great Britain, and the Soviet Union, see Hauner, "Afghanistan between the Great Powers, 1938–1945," *International Journal of Middle East Studies* 14 (November 1982): 481–99.

47. Adamec, *Afghanistan's Foreign Affairs*, 217–27, 238–43.

THREE

1. Louis Dupree, *Afghanistan* (1973; reprint, Oxford: Oxford University Press, 1997), 334–41.

2. Charles Evans Hughes to Warren G. Harding, July 18, 1921, *Papers Relating to the Foreign Relations of the United States, 1921* (Washington, DC: U.S. Department of State, 1936), 1:258 (hereafter *FRUS*), http://digicoll.library.wisc.edu/cgi-bin/FRUS/FRUS-idx?type=goto&id=FRUS.FRUS1921v01&isize=M&page=258. Also see Amin Saikal, *Modern Afghanistan: A History of Struggle and Survival* (New York: Palgrave Macmillan, 2004), 66.

3. Harding to Amanullah Khan, July 29, 1921, *FRUS, 1921*, 1:261, http://digicoll.library.wisc.edu/cgi-bin/FRUS/FRUS-idx?type=goto&id=FRUS.FRUS1921v01&isize=M&page=261.

4. "Proposal for the Establishment of Diplomatic and Consular Representation between the United States and Afghanistan," *FRUS, 1926*, 1:557–60, http://images.library.wisc.edu/FRUS/EFacs/1926v01/reference/frus.frus1926v01.i0007.pdf.

5. Leon B. Poullada and Leila D. J. Poullada, *The Kingdom of Afghanistan and the United States: 1828–1973* (Lincoln, NE: Center for Afghan Studies, University of Nebraska at Omaha, and Dageforde Publishing, 1995), 41–42; Ludwig W. Adamec, *Afghanistan, 1900–1923: A Diplomatic History* (Berkeley: University of California Press, 1967), 236.

6. Theodore Roosevelt Jr. and Kermit Roosevelt, *East of the Sun and West of the Moon* (New York: Blue Ribbon Books, 1926), 9. The brothers set out in May 1925 on an expedition for the Field Museum of Natural History in Chicago to procure a collection of wildlife from the Pamir and Tian Shan Mountains, including several specimen of *ovis poli*, a rare species of wild sheep, argali, first described by Marco Polo for European audiences. Theodore Roosevelt, "To the Roof of the World," *Boy's Life*, November 1926, 10–11, 61; Peter Collier, *The Roosevelts: An American Saga* (New York: Simon & Schuster, 1994), 302–8. For the Roosevelt brothers' impact on subsequent travel to the region, see William J. Morden, *Across Asia's Snows and Deserts* (New York: G. P. Putnam's Sons, 1927).

7. Mohammad Zahir Shah to Franklin D. Roosevelt, April 24, 1934, *FRUS, 1934*, 2:748, http://digicoll.library.wisc.edu/cgi-bin/FRUS/FRUS-idx?type=goto&id=FRUS.FRUS1934v02&isize=M&page=748.

8. William Phillips to Roosevelt, August 21, 1934, *FRUS, 1934*, 2:749, http://digicoll.library.wisc.edu/cgi-bin/FRUS/FRUS-idx?type=turn&entity=FRUS.FRUS1934v02.p0849&id=FRUS.FRUS1934v02&isize=M.

9. Roosevelt to Zahir Shah, August 21, 1934, *FRUS, 1934*, 2:750, http://digicoll. library.wisc.edu/cgi-bin/FRUS/FRUS-idx?type=turn&entity=FRUS.FRUS1934v02. p0850&id=FRUS.FRUS1934v02&isize=M.

10. "Provisional Agreement regarding Friendship, Diplomatic, and Consular Representation between the United States and Afghanistan," March 26, 1936, 49 Stat. 3873, Executive Agreement Series 88, in Charles I. Bevans, comp., *Treaties and Other International Agreements of the United States of America, 1776–1949*, Vol. 5: *Afghanistan-Burma* (Washington, DC: U.S. Department of State, 1970), 1–2. See also discussion related to the agreement in *FRUS, 1936*, 3:1–7, http:// images.library.wisc.edu/FRUS/EFacs/1936v03/reference/frus.frus1936v03.i0005.pdf.

11. Leon Poullada also mentioned negotiations between the A. J. Alsdorf Corporation of Chicago and the Afghan government for tanks, armored cars, and howitzers. Poullada and Poullada, *Afghanistan and the United States*, 128.

12. See correspondence in *FRUS, 1937*, 2:597–614, http://images.library.wisc.edu/FRUS/ EFacs/1937v02/reference/frus.frus1937v02.i0024.pdf. This deal, which was three years in the making, was finalized in Berlin without the participation, and largely without the knowledge, of the U.S. government.

13. Memorandum, Wallace S. Murray to Cordell Hull, May 7, 1938, *FRUS, 1938*, 2:752–53, http://digicoll.library.wisc.edu/cgi-bin/FRUS/FRUS-idx?type=goto&id=FRUS. FRUS1938v02&isize=M&page=752.

14. John A. DeNovo, *American Interests and Policies in the Middle East, 1900–1939* (Minneapolis: University of Minnesota Press, 1963), 314–15; Kristen Blake, *The U.S.-Soviet Confrontation in Iran, 1945–1962: A Case in the Annals of the Cold War* (Lanham, MD: University Press of America, 2009), 15–16; Stephen L. McFarland, "A Peripheral View of the Origins of the Cold War: The Crisis in Iran, 1941–1947," *Diplomatic History* 4 (Fall 1980): 333–51; Olaf K. Caroe, *Wells of Power: The Oilfields of South-Western Asia: A Regional and Global Study* (London: Macmillan, 1951).

15. Wallace S. Murray, "American Diplomatic Representation in Afghanistan," July 27, 1937, *FRUS, 1937*, 2:610, http://digicoll.library.wisc.edu/cgi-bin/FRUS/FRUS-idx?type=goto&id=FRUS.FRUS1937v02&isize=M&page=610.

16. Louis G. Dreyfus Jr. to Hull, June 27, 1941, *FRUS, 1941*, 3:259, http://digicoll.library. wisc.edu/cgi-bin/FRUS/FRUS-idx?type=goto&id=FRUS.FRUS1941v03&isize=M&page=259.

17. See discussion in *FRUS, 1941*, 3:255–63, http://images.library.wisc.edu/FRUS/ EFacs/1941v03/reference/frus.frus1941v03.i0008.pdf.

18. Cornelius Van H. Engert, *A Report on Afghanistan* (Washington, DC: U.S. Government Printing Office, 1924). For Engert's trip and the State Department's response to his lengthy report (225 published pages), see Poullada and Poullada, *Afghanistan and the United States*, 15–17.

19. Engert to Hull, July 25, 1942, *FRUS, 1942*, 4:51, http://digicoll.library.wisc.edu/ cgi-bin/FRUS/FRUS-idx?type=goto&id=FRUS.FRUS1942v04&isize=M&page=51.

20. "Reply of the President (Roosevelt) to the Remarks of the Minister of Afghanistan (Aziz), July 4, 1943," in Leland M. Goodrich and Marie J. Carroll, eds., *Documents on American Foreign Relations*, Vol. 5: *July 1942–June 1943* (Boston, MA: World Peace Foundation, 1944), 605. Roosevelt stated: "You will find, I am sure, Mr. Minister, that the love of freedom upon which we in the United States so pride ourselves is similar to your own and that there is much in the mutual idealism of our two peoples to cement the friendship now being manifest."

21. Engert to Hull, November 6, 1943, *FRUS, 1943*, 4:32, http://digicoll.library.wisc. edu/cgi-bin/FRUS/FRUS-idx?type=goto&id=FRUS.FRUS1943v04&isize=M&page=32.

22. Ibid.

23. Engert to Hull, February 14, 1943, *FRUS, 1943*, 4:21, http://digicoll.library.wisc. edu/cgi-bin/FRUS/FRUS-idx?type=goto&id=FRUS.FRUS1943v04&isize=M&page=21.

For Afghanistan's balancing of German, Soviet, and British interests, see Ludwig W. Adamec, *Afghanistan's Foreign Affairs to the Mid-Twentieth Century: Relations with the USSR, Germany, and Britain* (Tucson: University of Arizona Press, 1974), 244–47, 262–63.

24. Engert to Hull, April 29, 1943, *FRUS, 1943*, 4:23, http://digicoll.library.wisc.edu/cgi-bin/FRUS/FRUS-idx?type=turn&entity=FRUS.FRUS1943v04.p0035&id=FRUS.FRUS1943v04&isize=M.

25. Hull to Engert, November 23, 1943, *FRUS, 1943*, 4:34–35, http://digicoll.library.wisc.edu/cgi-bin/FRUS/FRUS-idx?type=goto&id=FRUS.FRUS1943v04&isize=M&page=34.

26. "Karakul Sheep," *Life*, July 16, 1945, 65–68; Ali Mohammad, "Karakul as the Most Important Article of Afghan Trade," *Afghanistan* (Kabul), 4 (December 1949): 48–53.

27. Harold R. Maddux to Wallace S. Murray, "Suggestion by Military Attaché that a U.S. Military Mission be Sent to Afghanistan," June 12, 1944, in Poullada and Poullada, *Afghanistan and the United States*, appendix 4.

28. Engert to Hull, August 7, 1942, *FRUS, 1942*, 4:54, http://digicoll.library.wisc.edu/cgi-bin/FRUS/FRUS-idx?type=goto&id=FRUS.FRUS1942v04&isize=M&page=54.

29. Engert to Hull, May 27, 1943, *FRUS, 1943*, 4:25, http://digicoll.library.wisc.edu/cgi-bin/FRUS/FRUS-idx?type=goto&id=FRUS.FRUS1943v04&isize=M&page=25.

30. The group included Lt. Gen. Mohammad Daud Khan, Kabul Army Corps; Lt. Gen. Muhammad Umar Khan, Afghan army; Col. Muhd Ali Khan, signals officer; Maj. Abdur Razak Khan, Afghan air force; Maj. Abdul Ghaffar Khan, cavalry officer; and Maj. Muhd Nasim Khan, artillery officer. *History of the XX Bomber Command*, December 1944, Air Force Historical Research Agency, reel A7757, frames 10–12.

31. Jacob C. Hurewitz, *Middle East Politics: The Military Dimension* (New York: Praeger, for Council on Foreign Relations, 1969), 301.

32. Memorandum of Conversation, Washington, DC, November 19, 1948, *FRUS, 1948*, 5:492 (first quote), http://digicoll.library.wisc.edu/cgi-bin/FRUS/FRUS-idx?type=goto&id=FRUS.FRUS1948v05p1&isize=M&page=492; Memorandum of Conversation, Washington, DC, December 8, 1948, *FRUS, 1948*, 5:493 (second quote), http://digicoll.library.wisc.edu/cgi-bin/FRUS/FRUS-idx?type=goto&id=FRUS.FRUS1948v05p1&isize=M&submit=Go+to+page&page=493.

33. Henry S. Bradsher, *Afghanistan and the Soviet Union* (Durham, NC: Duke University Press, 1983), 19.

34. Poullada and Poullada, *Afghanistan and the United States*, 4.

35. The U.S. military did provide some noncombat equipment at the end of the war. The State-Army-Navy-Air Force Coordinating Committee (SANACC), the precursor to the National Security Council, argued, "For all practical purposes Afghanistan is almost totally dependent on foreign sources for its military requirements. Up to now the Afghan Army has obtained from the U.S. only surplus hospital and non-combatant equipment, through the purchase for cash of U.S. surplus property in India in 1945." See SANACC 360/14, "Appraisal of U.S. National Interests in South Asia," April 19, 1949, *FRUS, 1949*, 6:23, http://digicoll.library.wisc.edu/cgi-bin/FRUS/FRUS-idx?type=goto&id=FRUS.FRUS1949v06&isize=M&page=23.

36. Jeffrey J. Roberts, *The Origins of Conflict in Afghanistan* (Westport, CT: Praeger, 2003), 74–75.

37. Ibid., 120.

38. Daniel Balland, "Boundaries of Afghanistan," in Ehsan Yarshater, ed., *Encyclopedia Iranica* (London: Routledge, 1982), 4:406–15, online at http://www.iranicaonline.org/articles/boundaries-iii.

39. Leon B. Poullada, *Reform and Rebellion in Afghanistan, 1919–1929: King Amanullah's Failure to Modernize a Tribal Society* (Ithaca, NY: Cornell University Press, 1973), 29; see also William Kerr Fraser-Tytler, *Afghanistan: A Study of Political Developments in Central and Southern Asia*, 3d ed. (New York: Oxford University Press, 1967).

40. Letter from South East Asia Department to Chancery, April 28, 1949, in Ludwig W. Adamec, *Historical Dictionary of Afghanistan*, 3d ed. (Lanham, MD: Scarecrow Press, 2003), 407.

41. For U.S. official sources on the "Pushtunistan Dispute," see *FRUS, 1952–54*, 11:1365–1498, http://digicoll.library.wisc.edu/cgi-bin/FRUS/FRUS-idx?type=goto&id=FRUS.FRUS1 95254v11p2&isize=M&page=1365; *FRUS, 1955–57*, 8:163–258, http://digicoll.library.wisc. edu/cgi-bin/FRUS/FRUS-idx?type=goto&id=FRUS.FRUS195557v08&isize=M&page=163. For an Afghan official tract, see Rahman Pazhwak, *An Article on Pakhtunistan, a New State in Central Asia* (London: Royal Afghan Embassy, 1960). Also see Saikal, *Modern Afghanistan*, 122–23, 130–34; Bradsher, *Afghanistan and the Soviet Union*, 25–26; Victoria Schofield, *Afghan Frontier: At the Crossroads of Conflict*, rev. ed. (London: Tauris Parke, 2010), 258–64; Husain Haqqani, *Pakistan: Between Mosque and Military* (Washington, DC: Carnegie Endowment for International Peace, 2005), 159–76; Rizwan Hussain, *Pakistan and the Emergence of Islamic Militancy in Afghanistan* (Burlington, VT: Ashgate, 2005), 61–82.

42. On January 1, 1950, Pakistan blockaded fuel trucks destined for Afghanistan. It repeated this action in 1953, 1955, and 1961. Martin Ewans, *Afghanistan: A Short History of Its People and Politics* (New York: Perennial, 2002), 158; Edward Girardet, *Afghanistan: The Soviet War* (New York: St. Martin's, 1985), 95; Daveed Gartenstein-Ross and Tara Vassefi, "The Forgotten History of Afghanistan-Pakistan Relations," *Yale Journal of International Affairs* 7 (March 2012): 38–45, http://yalejournal.org/wp-content/uploads/2012/04/Article-Gartenstein_Ross-and-Vassefi.pdf.

43. Khushal Khan Khattak (1613–89) was a *malik*, or chief, and warrior-poet who advocated for Afghan unity (in this case, Pashto speakers) to overthrow their Mughal rulers. Adamec, *Historical Dictionary of Afghanistan*, 220–21.

44. Poullada and Poullada, *Afghanistan and the United States*, 99.

45. Department of State Policy Statement, "United States Policy with Respect to Afghanistan," February 21, 1951, *FRUS, 1951*, 6:2008–9, http://digicoll.library.wisc.edu/ cgi-bin/FRUS/FRUS-idx?type=goto&id=FRUS.FRUS1951v06p2&isize=M&page=2008. Diplomat-turned-scholar Leon Poullada much later observed that "the Pushtunistan dispute was the loose thread in the fabric of Afghan independence. The Soviets skillfully pulled this thread and unraveled Afghan freedom." Poullada and Poullada, *Afghanistan and the United States*, 82.

46. Dean G. Acheson to Embassy in Afghanistan, September 29, 1952, *FRUS, 1952–54*, 11:1456, http://history.state.gov/historicaldocuments/frus1952-54v11p2/d887; Charles Little to Department of State, July 10, 1954, *FRUS, 1952–54*, 11:1412–1413, http://history. state.gov/historicaldocuments/frus1952-54v11p2/d856. For more background on U.S.-Pakistan relations on these issues, see Haqqani, *Pakistan*, 162–65; Hussain, *Pakistan*, 68–72.

47. John E. Horner to Department of State, October 2, 1952, *FRUS, 1952–54*, 11:1457, http://history.state.gov/historicaldocuments/frus1952-54v11p2/d888. For the Afghan views, see Saikal, *Modern Afghanistan*, 123–24; for the Pakistani side, see Hussain, *Pakistan*, 69–71.

48. National Security Council, "United States Objectives and Policies with Respect to the Near East," July 23, 1954, NSC 5428, *FRUS, 1952–54*, 9:527, http://history.state.gov/ historicaldocuments/frus1952-54v09p1/d219. This amended the original policies of NSC 155/1, following developments that included a change of power in Iran, the visit of Vice President Richard M. Nixon to the region, and successful Pakistani lobbying for military aid.

49. James S. Lay Jr., "United States Objectives and Policies with Respect to the Near East," Memorandum for the National Security Council, July 6, 1954, p. 23, para. 29 c, available through the National Security Archive, http://www.gwu.edu/~nsarchiv/NSAEBB/ NSAEBB78/propaganda%20126.pdf.

50. This sentiment was shared by the British since the mid-nineteenth century. It was then reinforced by the British Committee of Imperial Defence at the turn of the twentieth

century. See Christopher M. Wyatt, *Afghanistan and the Defence of Empire: Diplomacy and Strategy during the Great Game* (London: I. B. Tauris, 2011), 91–101.

51. Balland, "Boundaries of Afghanistan." The signing of the first transit agreements between Afghanistan and the USSR on July 17, 1950, and between Afghanistan and Iran on December 3, 1960, coincided with periods of heightened border tension with Pakistan. Paul Robinson and Jay Dixon explained that the Soviet treaty "provided for an exchange of agricultural products in return for Soviet petroleum, cotton, cloth, sugar and other commodities. In addition, the agreement provided for duty-free transit of Afghan goods over Soviet territory," in *Aiding Afghanistan: A History of Soviet Assistance to a Developing Country* (New York: Columbia University Press, 2013), 49.

52. Balland noted that there was an eight-week period from January to March 1962 when the import of American aid supplies to Afghanistan was permitted. Balland, "Boundaries of Afghanistan."

FOUR

1. Henry Cabot Lodge Jr. to John Foster Dulles, October 12, 1954, *Foreign Relations of the United States, 1952–1954* (Washington, DC: U.S. Department of State, 1983), 11:1423 (hereafter *FRUS*), http://history.state.gov/historicaldocuments/frus1952-54v11p2/d864.

2. Henry A. Byroade, "Soviet Démarche to Afghanistan," October 10, 1952, *FRUS, 1952–54*, 11:1458–61, http://history.state.gov/historicaldocuments/frus1952-54v11p2/d889.

3. John E. Horner to Department of State, October 2, 1952, *FRUS, 1952–54*, 11:1456, http://history.state.gov/historicaldocuments/frus1952-54v11p2/d888.

4. See Nake M. Kamrany, *Peaceful Competition in Afghanistan: American and Soviet Models for Economic Aid* (Washington, DC: Communication Service Corporation, 1969), for a close read of U.S. and Soviet aid to Afghanistan during the 1950s and 1960s. The Helmand River Valley project is discussed in the next chapter.

5. Horner to Department of State, September 23, 1952, *FRUS, 1952–54*, 11:1453, http://history.state.gov/historicaldocuments/frus1952-54v11p2/d886.

6. Amin Saikal, *Modern Afghanistan: A History of Struggle and Survival* (New York: Palgrave Macmillan, 2004), 120–21.

7. National Intelligence Estimate, "Outlook for Afghanistan," October 19, 1954, *FRUS, 1952–54*, 11:1482, http://history.state.gov/historicaldocuments/frus1952-54v11p2/d905. See also Harry N. Howard, "The Regional Pacts and the Eisenhower Doctrine," *Annals of the American Academy of Political and Social Science* 401 (May 1972): 85–94.

8. Angus I. Ward to Department of State, December 15, 1953, *FRUS, 1952–54*, 11:1407, http://history.state.gov/historicaldocuments/frus1952-54v11p2/d85; Richard M. Nixon, Report to National Security Council, December 23, 1953, *FRUS, 1952–54*, 11:1407n, http://history.state.gov/historicaldocuments/frus1952-54v11p2/d852.

9. Henry A. Byroade, "The Changing Position of Afghanistan in Asia," Department of State *Bulletin*, January 23, 1961, 125, 127 (hereafter DOS *Bulletin*; full archive online at http://www.bpl.org/govinfo/online-collections/federal-executive-branch/department-of-state-bulletin-1939-1989/).

10. National Intelligence Estimate, "Outlook for Afghanistan," October 19, 1954, *FRUS, 1952–54*, 11:1481–97 (quote p. 1483), http://history.state.gov/historicaldocuments/frus1952-54v11p2/d905. This analysis ultimately proved accurate. See Nake M. Kamrany, *The Six Stages in the Sovietization of Afghanistan* (Boulder, CO: Economic Institute for Research and Education, 1983), 3–9, on the systematic Soviet economic and cultural penetration of Afghanistan.

11. See R. K. Ramazani, "Afghanistan and the USSR," *Middle East Journal* 12 (Spring 1958): 144–52.

12. Mohammad Daud was ultimately an expansionist and sought the return of Pashtun lands to the east and Baluch lands to the south. Saikal, *Modern Afghanistan*, 115–16, 181.

13. See "Pushtunistan Dispute," *FRUS, 1955–57*, 8:163–258 (http://history.state.gov/historicaldocuments/frus1955-57v08/ch4), for extensive materials on a range of topics, including mob confrontation of two Americans in Kabul and on the impact of this conflict between Afghanistan and Pakistan.

14. Leon B. Poullada and Leila D. J. Poullada, *The Kingdom of Afghanistan and the United States: 1828–1973* (Lincoln, NE: Center for Afghan Studies, University of Nebraska at Omaha, and Dageforde Publishing, 1995), 104; Daveed Gartenstein-Ross and Tara Vassefi, "The Forgotten History of Afghanistan-Pakistan Relations," *Yale Journal of International Affairs* 7 (March 2012): 41–42, http://yalejournal.org/wp-content/uploads/2012/04/Article-Gartenstein_Ross-and-Vassefi.pdf.

15. Horace A. Hildreth to Department of State, May 6, 1955, *FRUS, 1955–57*, 8:182–83, http://history.state.gov/historicaldocuments/frus1955-57v08/d89.

16. Martin Ewans, *Afghanistan: A Short History of Its People and Politics* (New York: Perennial, 2002), 154–56.

17. Louis Dupree, *Afghanistan* (1973; reprint, Oxford: Oxford University Press, 1997), 508; Ewans, *Afghanistan*, 156; Jacob C. Hurewitz, *Middle East Politics: The Military Dimension* (New York: Praeger, for Council on Foreign Relations, 1969), 301. Khrushchev declared that "we trade less for economic than for political reasons." Paul Robinson and Jay Dixon, *Aiding Afghanistan: A History of Soviet Assistance to a Developing Country* (New York: Columbia University Press, 2013), 51.

18. Nikita S. Khrushchev, *Khrushchev Remembers*, trans. and ed. Strobe Talbott (Boston, MA: Little, Brown, 1970), 508. See also Ewans, *Afghanistan*, 157; Robinson and Dixon, *Aiding Afghanistan*, 51.

19. Alam Payind, "Soviet-Afghan Relations from Cooperation to Occupation," *International Journal of Middle East Studies* 21 (February 1989): 113.

20. Henry S. Bradsher, *Afghanistan and the Soviet Union* (Durham, NC: Duke University Press, 1983), 24.

21. Eva Grenbäck, *Arms Trade Registers: The Arms Trade with the Third World* (Cambridge, MA: MIT Press, 1975), 32; Wynfred Joshua and Stephen P. Gibert, *Arms for the Third World: Soviet Military Aid Diplomacy* (Baltimore, MD: Johns Hopkins University Press, 1969), 56–57.

22. Saikal, *Modern Afghanistan*, 126; Payind, "Soviet-Afghan Relations," 112.

23. Harvey H. Smith, *Area Handbook for Afghanistan* (Washington, DC: U.S. Government Printing Office, 1969), 378.

24. Patrick J. Garrity, "The Soviet Military Stake in Afghanistan, 1956–1979," *Journal of the Royal United Services Institute for Defence Studies* 125 (September 1980): 31–36; Kamrany, *Six Stages*, 9–10.

25. Donald N. Wilber, ed., *Afghanistan* (New Haven, CT: Human Relations Area Files, 1956), 185.

26. National Intelligence Estimate, "Probable Developments in Afghanistan's International Position," January 10 1956, *FRUS, 1955–57*, 8:218, http://history.state.gov/historicaldocuments/frus1955-57v08/d111.

27. Ibid., 8:217–19, http://history.state.gov/historicaldocuments/frus1955-57v08/d111.

28. Sheldon T. Mills to Department of State, January 3, 1958, *FRUS, 1958–60*, 15:216, http://history.state.gov/historicaldocuments/frus1958-60v15/d100.

29. Bradsher, *Afghanistan and the Soviet Union*, 28–31; Saikal, *Modern Afghanistan*, 130.

30. For the Soviet preference for credits to minimize corruption, see Robinson and Dixon, *Aiding Afghanistan*, 128–29.

31. Byroade, "Changing Position of Afghanistan in Asia," 133; Dupree, *Afghanistan*, 526–30. On the other hand, Kamrany noted coexistence and even unintentional cooperation between Americans and Soviets on the ground in Afghanistan during the 1950s and 1960s. From a U.S. policy perspective, however, competition with the Soviets in Afghanistan was a concern, and aid projects were a political tool. Kamrany, *Peaceful Competition in Afghanistan*, 17, 58, 86–89, 104.

32. "Export-Import Bank Loan to Afghanistan," DOS *Bulletin*, May 31, 1954, 836. The $21 million in 1949 equates to $206 million in 2013 dollars, while the $18.5 million from 1954 would be approximately $160 million. See also Kamrany, *Peaceful Competition in Afghanistan*, 23.

33. Memorandum on Afghanistan, Allen W. Dulles to John Foster Dulles, August 6, 1956, *FRUS, 1955–57*, 8:242, http://history.state.gov/historicaldocuments/frus1955-57v08/d121. The U.S. government initially pledged $14.8 million to develop air transport facilities to reduce dependence on Soviet air routes. *American Foreign Policy Current Documents, 1956* (Washington, DC: U.S. Department of State, 1959), 1303 (hereafter *AFP Current Docs*).

34. In a related move to generate public support, the International Cooperation Administration (ICA) announced that it had contracted an aircraft from Pan American to make fifteen to twenty round-trip flights from Kandahar to Jeddah over a sixty-day period to help Ariana, the Afghan airline, transport pilgrims performing hajj. "U.S. Will Help Transport Afghan Pilgrims to Mecca," DOS *Bulletin*, July 2, 1956, 25.

35. "ICA Aid to South Asia in Fiscal Year 1956," DOS *Bulletin*, September 24, 1956, 494.

36. "March 1960" Report, March 31, 1960, Reports, Program Reports, ICA/Morrison-Knudsen Contracts, Project Files Relating to Transportation, 1954–1961, Records of U.S. Foreign Assistance Agencies, 1942–1963, Record Group 469, National Archives. See also Yuri V. Bossin, "The Afghan Experience with International Assistance," in John D. Montgomery and Dennis A. Rondinelli, eds., *Beyond Reconstruction in Afghanistan: Lessons from Development Experience* (New York: Palgrave Macmillan, 2004), 83.

37. "U.S. Helps Afghan Airline Acquire Plane for Fleet," DOS *Bulletin*, May 23, 1960, 831. Also, Robert M. Snyder of the U.S. Operations Mission in Afghanistan gave a speech in Kabul on October 29, 1958, that outlined ICA technical and economic assistance in agriculture, mining, education, and road and air transportation. Snyder, "What ICA is Doing in Afghanistan," Department of State Publication 6671 (Washington, DC: U.S. Government Printing Office, 1959).

38. Ewans, *Afghanistan*, 159.

39. Mohammad Ali, *Afghanistan, The Mohammedzai Period: A Political History of the Country since the Beginning of the Nineteenth Century with Emphasis on its Foreign Relations* (Kabul: Kabul University Press, 1959), 201–2.

40. Ambassador Sheldon T. Mills reported that "Afghanistan's foreign policy as it relates to position in struggle between free world and Communist bloc is no longer fixed in pattern of close collaboration with Soviet which was evidence of Khrushchev-Bulganin visit, December 1955, but now is in state of flux." Mills to Department of State, January 3, 1958, *FRUS, 1958–60*, 15:215, http://history.state.gov/historicaldocuments/frus1958-60v15/d100.

41. Joint statement by Eisenhower and Daud, Washington, DC, June 27, 1958, *AFP Current Docs, 1958*, 1067–68.

42. Memorandum of Conversation, Department of State, Washington, DC, June 24, 1958, *FRUS, 1958–60*, 15:227, http://history.state.gov/historicaldocuments/frus1958-60v15/d108.

43. Eisenhower described the trip in his memoir, *The White House Years: Waging Peace, 1956–1961* (Garden City, NY: Doubleday, 1965), 497–99. He spent relatively little time in Afghanistan compared with stops in India (five days) and Pakistan (three days).

44. Memorandum of Conversation, Kabul, Afghanistan, December 9, 1959, *FRUS, 1958–60*, 15:321–25, http://history.state.gov/historicaldocuments/frus1958-60v15/d151.

45. Dwight D. Eisenhower, "Remarks Upon Arrival at Bagram Airport, Kabul," December 9, 1959, *Public Papers of the Presidents of the United States: Dwight D. Eisenhower, 1959* (Washington, DC: U.S. Government Printing Office, 1960), 821, http://quod.lib.umich.edu/p/ppotpus/4728423.1959.001/867?rgn=full+text;view=image.

46. Dwight D. Eisenhower, "Toast of the President at a Luncheon Given in His Honor by King Mohammad Zahir," Kabul, Afghanistan, December 9, 1959, ibid., 822–23, http://quod.lib.umich.edu/p/ppotpus/4728423.1959.001/868?rgn=full+text;view=image.

47. The business elements of the trip were expressed in a joint statement: "President Eisenhower gave assurances of the American desire to continue to assist Afghanistan in its task of strengthening its economic and social structure." "Joint Communique, Kabul, December 9," DOS *Bulletin*, December 28, 1959, 934.

48. Eisenhower, *Waging Peace*, 497.

49. Ibid., 498.

50. Memorandum of Conversation, Madrid, Spain, December 22, 1959, *FRUS, 1958–60*, 15:327, http://history.state.gov/historicaldocuments/frus1958-60v15/d153.

FIVE

1. There are several extensive online collections that include documents related to development efforts in the Helmand River Valley covered in this section: Kabul University/University of Arizona Afghanistan Digital Collections (http://www.afghandata.org:8080/xmlui/handle/azu/1); Oregon State University Middle East Water Collection (http://oregondigital.org/digcol/mewaters/); Oregon State University Transboundary Freshwater Dispute Database (http://ocid.nacse.org/tfdd/); and a collection posted by a retired analyst from the U.S. Agency for International Development (http://scottshelmandvalleyarchives.org/).

2. Lloyd Baron, "Sector Analysis: Helmand-Arghandab Valley Region," U.S. Agency for International Development, February 1973, typescript, Library of Congress, 7, http://www.afghandata.org:8080/xmlui/bitstream/handle/azu/531/azu_acku_pamphlet_hd2065_6_b37_1973_w.pdf; Louis Dupree, *Afghanistan* (1973; reprint, Oxford: Oxford University Press, 1997), 482.

3. *Report on Development of Helmand Valley, Afghanistan* (Washington, DC: Tudor Engineering Company, 1956), http://www.afghandata.org:8080/xmlui/bitstream/handle/azu/524/azu_acku_pamphlet_hd1698_a3_r4_1956_w.pdf.

4. For an overview and key context connecting these efforts to the later developments that led to the attacks of September 11, 2001, see Nick Cullather, "Damming Afghanistan: Modernization in a Buffer State," *Journal of American History* 89 (September 2002): 512–37; for the full scope of U.S. aid to the project, which continued until 1979, see Cynthia Clapp-Wincek and Emily Baldwin, *The Helmand Valley Project in Afghanistan* (Washington, DC: U.S. Agency for International Development, 1983), http://scottshelmandvalleyarchives.org/docs/evl-83-02.pdf.

5. *New York Times*, August 9, 1946, 5.

6. Nake M. Kamrany, *Peaceful Competition in Afghanistan: American and Soviet Models for Economic Aid* (Washington, DC: Communication Service Corporation, 1969), 31, 34; Cullather, "Damning Afghanistan," 520–27 (quote p. 524).

7. Louis G. Dreyfus Jr. to Dean G. Acheson, September 19, 1949, *Foreign Relations of the United States, 1949* (Washington, DC: U.S. Department of State, 1977), 6:1778 (hereafter *FRUS*), http://images.library.wisc.edu/FRUS/EFacs/1949v06/reference/frus.frus1949v06.i0016.pdf.

8. Amin Saikal, *Modern Afghanistan: A History of Struggle and Survival* (New York: Palgrave Macmillan, 2004), 109; Dupree, *Afghanistan*, 484. Zabuli founded the Afghan national bank and played a significant role in Afghan economic development from the 1930s through the 1950s. For background on Zabuli's political and commercial significance, see Saikal, *Modern Afghanistan*, 109, 163; for details on Zabuli's larger economic plan, see Kamrany, *Peaceful Competition in Afghanistan*, 24.

9. It was expanded and renamed the Helmand-Arghandab Valley Authority (HAVA) in 1965.

10. Daniel Balland, "Arghandab River," in Ehsan Yarshater, ed., *Encyclopedia Iranica* (London: Routledge, 1982), 2:398–400, http://www.iranicaonline.org/articles/argandab-river. The Dahla Dam was originally known as the Arghandab Dam.

11. "Four Point Programs—Afghanistan," Department of State *Bulletin*, July 14, 1952, 62 (hereafter DOS *Bulletin*; full archive online at http://www.bpl.org/govinfo/online-collections/federal-executive-branch/department-of-state-bulletin-1939-1989/). Kamrany, *Peaceful Competition in Afghanistan*, 25–26, provides some context on the Point Four Program in Afghanistan, signed with Kabul on February 7, 1951.

12. "Export-Import Bank Loan to Afghanistan," DOS *Bulletin*, May 31, 1954, 836.

13. N. H. Kirk, "Status of the Eximbank Loan to Afghanistan," August 11, 1953, *FRUS, 1952–54*, 11:1466–70, http://history.state.gov/historicaldocuments/frus1952-54v11p2/d895. Recent experiences of NATO Provincial Reconstruction Teams indicate how important these local relationships can be to a project's success.

14. N. H. Kirk, "Status of the Eximbank Loan to Afghanistan," August 11, 1953, *FRUS, 1952–54*, 11:1469, http://history.state.gov/historicaldocuments/frus1952-54v11p2/d895.

15. John Foster Dulles to Horace A. Hildreth, July 12, 1955, *FRUS, 1955–57*, 8:189, http://history.state.gov/historicaldocuments/frus1955-57v08/d93. Cullather argued that "to the Eisenhower administration, Morrison Knudsen's outpost in Kandahar was the scientific frontier of American power in Central Asia." Cullather, "Damning Afghanistan," 528.

16. Peter G. Franck, "Technical Assistance through the United Nations: The U.N. Mission in Afghanistan, 1950–1963," in Howard M. Teaf and Peter G. Franck, *Hands Across Frontiers: Case Studies in International Cooperation* (Ithaca, NY: Cornell University Press, 1955), 13–61 (quote p. 36); Dupree, *Afghanistan*, 483.

17. *Report on Development of Helmand Valley, Afghanistan*, i, 5, 189–93; "Afghanistan Reclamation Project Expected to Produce Added Income," DOS *Bulletin*, August 19, 1957, 315–16.

18. Kamrany, *Peaceful Competition in Afghanistan*, 31, 34.

19. See Cullather, "Damning Afghanistan," 529–30, for the ethnic and political implications; see also Dupree, *Afghanistan*, 503–4. The villages were ultimately abandoned by 1960 due to poor soil conditions, but during the early years of the project, there was palpable enthusiasm for it within the U.S. government. Kamrany, *Peaceful Competition in Afghanistan*, 36, mentions that 1,330 families moved as part of this project.

20. Aloys Arthur Michel, *The Kabul, Kunduz, and Helmand Valleys and the National Economy of Afghanistan: A Study of Regional Resources and the Comparative Advantages of Development* (Washington, DC: National Academy of Sciences, 1959), 425.

21. Ibid.

22. Kamrany, *Peaceful Competition in Afghanistan*, 32. The seven objectives were: 1) to provide new farms for nomads and landless villagers; 2) to raise the standard of living of peoples in the valley; 3) to produce agricultural and manufactured products for export; 4) to develop electric power; 5) to create government income to eventually pay off the

investment; 6) to provide protection against floods; and 7) to provide early uses of all waters of the Helmand River except that portion to which Iran was entitled. Kamrany, *Peaceful Competition in Afghanistan*, 29.

23. Henry A. Byroade to Department of State, April 14, 1959, *FRUS, 1958–60*, 15:266, http://history.state.gov/historicaldocuments/frus1958-60v15/d126.

24. Henry A. Byroade, "The Changing Position of Afghanistan in Asia," DOS *Bulletin*, January 23, 1961, 130 (first quote); Dean Rusk to Embassy in Afghanistan, January 25, 1963, *FRUS, 1961–63*, 19:483 (second quote), http://history.state.gov/historicaldocuments/frus1961-63v19/d246. For continuing U.S. aid, see Clapp-Wincek and Baldwin, *Helmand Valley Project in Afghanistan*.

25. Samuel M. Burke and Lawrence Ziring, eds., *Pakistan's Foreign Policy: An Historical Analysis*, 2d ed. (Karachi: Oxford University Press, 1990), 147–73; Farooq N. Bajwa, *Pakistan and the West: The First Decade, 1947–1957* (Karachi: Oxford University Press, 1996), 55–95; Shuja Nawaz, *Crossed Swords: Pakistan, Its Army, and the Wars Within* (Karachi: Oxford University Press, 2008), 92–121.

26. The latter was striking since Afghanistan had always been an agricultural exporter before the 1950s.

27. Ambassador Chester B. Bowles wrote to Dulles on December 30, 1953: "I believe we will isolate Pakistan, draw the Soviet Union certainly into Afghanistan and probably into India, eliminate the possibility of Pakistan-Indian or Pakistan-Afghan rapprochement, further jeopardize the outlook for the Indian Five Year Plan, increase the dangerous wave of anti-Americanism throughout India and other South Asian countries, open up explosive new opportunities for the Soviet Union, gravely weaken the hopes for stable democratic government in India, and add nothing whatsoever to our military strength in the area." Quoted from Bowles's personal papers in Robert J. McMahon, *The Cold War on the Periphery: The United States, India, and Pakistan* (New York: Columbia University Press, 1994), 174.

28. National Security Council, "Statement of Policy on U.S. Policy Toward South Asia," January 10, 1957, *FRUS, 1955–57*, 8:33–34, 37, 42, http://history.state.gov/historicaldocuments/frus1955-57v08/d5.

29. Memorandum of Conversation, Kabul, Afghanistan, December 9, 1959, *FRUS, 1958–60*, 15:324, http://history.state.gov/historicaldocuments/frus1958-60v15/d151. This comment was repeated during Naim's visit with Eisenhower eight months later. Memorandum of Conversation, New York, NY, September 23, 1960, ibid., 15:356, http://history.state.gov/historicaldocuments/frus1958-60v15/d171.

30. Richard Gott, ed., *Documents on International Affairs, 1960* (London: Oxford University Press, 1964), 483–86.

31. Editorial Note, *FRUS, 1958–60*, 15:359, http://history.state.gov/historicaldocuments/frus1958-60v15/d172.

32. Byroade to Department of State, September 29, 1960, ibid., 15:360–62, http://history.state.gov/historicaldocuments/frus1958-60v15/d173.

33. Dwight D. Eisenhower to Mohammad Zahir Shah, October 21, 1960, ibid., 15:366, http://history.state.gov/historicaldocuments/frus1958-60v15/d177.

34. Nikita S. Khrushchev, speech, March 6, 1960, Moscow, USSR, *American Foreign Policy Current Documents, 1960* (Washington, DC: U.S. Department of State, 1964), 501–2 (hereafter *AFP Current Docs*). Khrushchev viewed the Pashtunistan conflict as a means to pressure Pakistan for its ties to Washington. See Roby C. Barrett, *The Greater Middle East and the Cold War: U.S. Foreign Policy under Eisenhower and Kennedy* (London: I. B. Tauris, 2007), 403.

35. White House press release, October 17, 1961, and notes, *AFP Current Docs, 1961*, 692.

36. McMahon, *Cold War on the Periphery*, 267; Nawaz, *Crossed Swords*, 185–87; Burke and Ziring, *Pakistan's Foreign Policy*, 195–97.

37. Nawaz, *Crossed Swords*, 185. Peshawar Air Station in Badaber was later used as a training camp for Afghan mujahideen as part of Operation Cyclone, the CIA program to fund the mujahideen during the Soviet-Afghan war. Peter L. Bergen argues convincingly of the limited contact between CIA officers and Afghan and Arab mujahideen, as operational activities and training were ceded to Pakistan's Inter-Services Intelligence (ISI). Bergen, *Holy War, Inc.: Inside the Secret World of Osama bin Laden* (New York: Free Press, 2001), 65–66.

38. McMahon, *Cold War on the Periphery*, 320; Nawaz, *Crossed Swords*, 186–87. The base in Peshawar was the departure point of Francis Gary Powers's ill-fated U–2 mission on May 1, 1960.

39. Quoted in McMahon, *Cold War on the Periphery*, 320.

40. "Prime Minister of Afghanistan Visits the United States," DOS *Bulletin*, April 17, 1967, 627–31.

41. Jacob C. Hurewitz, *Middle East Politics: The Military Dimension* (New York: Praeger, for Council on Foreign Relations, 1969), 303.

42. There is no established source for this frequently cited remark.

43. Saikal, *Modern Afghanistan*, 174; Martin Ewans, *Afghanistan: A Short History of Its People and Politics* (New York: Perennial, 2002), 179; M. Hassan Kakar, "The Fall of the Afghan Monarchy in 1973," *International Journal of Middle East Studies* 9 (May 1978): 195–214.

44. Nawaz, *Crossed Swords*, 350–51; Burke and Ziring, *Pakistan's Foreign Policy*, 432–34.

45. Saikal, *Modern Afghanistan*, 181.

Six

1. Muhammad R. Azmi, "Soviet Politico-Military Penetration in Afghanistan, 1955 to 1979," *Armed Forces & Society* 12 (Spring 1986): 329–49; Vladimir Shlapentokh, *Soviet Intellectuals and Political Power: The Post-Stalin Era* (London: I. B. Tauris, 1990), 147–48. Earlier tradition is evident in John L. H. Keep, *Soldiers of the Tsar: Army and Society in Russia, 1462–1874* (Oxford: Clarendon Press, 1985), 231–72.

2. Quoted in Henry S. Bradsher, *Afghanistan and the Soviet Union* (Durham, NC: Duke University Press, 1983), 27.

3. An examination of the biographies of the leaders of the three effective coups reveals this. According to Alam Payind, the Soviet military trained 4,000 Afghan officers between 1956 and 1978. Payind, "Soviet-Afghan Relations from Cooperation to Occupation," *International Journal of Middle East Studies* 21 (February 1989): 112.

4. Military officers and coup leaders with direct Soviet ties included Pacha Gul Wafadar, Faiz Muhammad, Mohammad Rafi, Abdul Qadir Dagarwal, Abdul Hamid Muhtat, Mohammad Aslam Watanjar, Sherjan Mazdoryar, and Sayed Mohammad Gulabzoi. For discussion of the coup leaders, see Martin Ewans, *Afghanistan: A Short History of Its People and Politics* (New York: Perennial, 2002), 179–80; Amin Saikal, *Modern Afghanistan: A History of Struggle and Survival* (New York: Palgrave Macmillan, 2004), 175; Bradsher, *Afghanistan and the Soviet Union*, 56–57; Fred Halliday, "Revolution in Afghanistan," *New Left Review*, November–December 1978, 3–44.

5. See *The Military Balance, 1973–1974* (London: International Institute for Strategic Studies, 1973), 49; *The Military Balance, 1975–1976* (London: International Institute for Strategic Studies, 1975), 52; *The Military Balance, 1977–1978* (London: International Institute

for Strategic Studies, 1977), 55–56; *The Military Balance, 1979–1980* (London: International Institute for Strategic Studies, 1979), 62–63. This was the third time in a decade that the Soviets conferred military aid to Afghanistan: November 14, 1966; September 4, 1969; and May 22, 1973. See Vasilii S. Khristoforov, *Afganistan: Praviashchaia partiia i armiia (1978–1989)* [Afghanistan: The Ruling Party and the Army] (Moscow: Granitsa, 2009), 16.

6. Saikal, *Modern Afghanistan*, 178–84.

7. See Anthony Arnold, *Afghanistan's Two-Party Communism: Parcham and Khalq* (Stanford, CA: Hoover Institution Press, 1983).

8. Bradsher, *Afghanistan and the Soviet Union*, 59–66.

9. See ibid., 74–109, for an overview of the Saur Revolution.

10. Ibid., 77. This announcement was premature since the palace had not yet been captured.

11. Ewans, *Afghanistan*, 187.

12. Bradsher, *Afghanistan and the Soviet Union*, 76.

13. Ibid., 82–85.

14. Afghanistan Task Force, "Afghanistan: Soviet Invasion and U.S. Response" (Issue Brief IB80006, Congressional Research Service, Washington, DC, May 2, 1980), 3, http://digital.library.unt.edu/ark:/67531/metacrs8151/m1/1/high_res_d/IB80006_1980May02.pdf.

15. Thomas J. Barfield, *Afghanistan: A Cultural and Political History* (Princeton, NJ: Princeton University Press, 2010), 225–33.

16. On May 1, 1978, the PDPA announced the names of the twenty-one cabinet members of the new government. There were eleven Khalqi and ten Parcham party members. Four had received training in the Soviet Union and spoke Russian, yet almost all spoke English. There were nine Pashtuns, eight Tajiks, two Hazaras, and two Uzbeks. See Louis Dupree, "The Democratic Republic of Afghanistan, 1979: Rhetoric, Repression, Reforms, and Revolts" (Report No. 32, American Universities Field Staff, Hanover, NH, 1979), 2.

17. Bradsher, *Afghanistan and the Soviet Union*, 89.

18. Rosanne Klass, "Afghanistan: The Accords," *Foreign Affairs* 66 (Summer 1988): 934.

19. Bradsher, *Afghanistan and the Soviet Union*, 96.

20. Arnold, *Afghanistan's Two-Party Communism*, 61. U.S. Afghanistan expert Louis Dupree supported this argument in "A Communist Label is Unjustified," *New York Times*, May 20, 1978, 18.

21. Barnett R. Rubin, "Political Elites in Afghanistan: Rentier State Building, Rentier State Wrecking," *International Journal of Middle East Studies* 24 (February 1992): 77–99.

22. Edward Girardet, *Afghanistan: The Soviet War* (New York: St. Martin's, 1985), 105.

23. "The Kidnapping and Death of Ambassador Adolph Dubs, February 14, 1979, Kabul, Afghanistan" (Office of Security, U.S. Department of State, Washington, DC, 1980).

24. Harold H. Saunders, statement before subcommittee on Asian and Pacific Affairs, House Foreign Relations Committee, September 26, 1979, *American Foreign Policy: Basic Documents, 1977–1980* (Washington: U.S. Department of State, 1983), 809 (hereafter *AFP Basic Docs*).

25. Steve Coll, *Ghost Wars: The Secret History of the CIA, Afghanistan, and bin Laden, from the Soviet Invasion to September 10, 2001* (New York: Penguin, 2004), 42–46; Bradsher, *Afghanistan and the Soviet Union*, 99.

26. Christian Friedrich Ostermann, "New Evidence on the War in Afghanistan," *Cold War International History Project Bulletin* 14/15 (Winter 2003–Spring 2004): 139–40.

27. Gilles Dorronsoro, *Revolution Unending: Afghanistan, 1979 to the Present* (New York: Columbia University Press, 2005), 98–104.

28. Patrick J. Garrity, "The Soviet Military Stake in Afghanistan, 1956–1979," *Journal of the Royal United Services Institute for Defence Studies* 125 (September 1980): 34; *Washington Post*, May 10, 1979.

29. Quoted in Coll, *Ghost Wars*, 40.

30. Bradsher, *Afghanistan and the Soviet Union*, 102; Khristoforov, *Afganistan*, 27–28.

31. Bradsher, *Afghanistan and the Soviet Union*, 150–51.

32. Rodric Braithwaite, *Afgantsy: The Russians in Afghanistan, 1979–89* (New York: Oxford University Press, 2011), 55.

33. George Jacobs, "Afghanistan Forces: How Many Soviets Are There?" *Jane's Defence Weekly*, June 22, 1985, 1228–33. *Military Balance, 1979–80*, 106, noted that twenty-two Mi–8s, twenty PT–78s, and twelve Mi–24s were granted in March and April 1979.

34. Artemy M. Kalinovsky, *A Long Goodbye: The Soviet Withdrawal from Afghanistan* (Cambridge, MA: Harvard University Press, 2011), 19.

35. Taraki and Amin had considerable misgivings about Soviet intentions. See M. Hassan Kakar, *Afghanistan: The Soviet Invasion and the Afghan Response, 1979–1982* (Berkeley: University of California Press, 1995), 40–45.

36. Quoted in Robert F. Baumann, *Russian-Soviet Unconventional Wars in the Caucasus, Central Asia, and Afghanistan* (Fort Leavenworth, KS: Combat Studies Institute, 1993), 133.

37. Kalinovsky, *Long Goodbye*, 20–21; Bradsher, *Afghanistan and the Soviet Union*, 110–25.

38. Kalinovsky, *Long Goodbye*, 21; Odd Arne Westad, "Concerning the Situation in 'A': New Russian Evidence on the Soviet Intervention in Afghanistan," *Cold War International History Project Bulletin* 8–9 (Winter 1996–97): 128–32, http://www.wilsoncenter.org/sites/default/files/e-dossier_4.pdf.

39. Nake M. Kamrany, *The Six Stages in the Sovietization of Afghanistan* (Boulder, CO: Economic Institute for Research and Education, 1983), 14. On mujahideen ideology, see Robert Johnson, *The Afghan Way of War: How and Why They Fight* (New York: Oxford University Press, 2011), 205–47.

40. Louis Dupree, *Afghanistan* (1973; reprint, Oxford: Oxford University Press, 1997), 776–77.

41. Saikal, *Modern Afghanistan*, 198.

42. Vladimir Snegirev and Valery Samunin, *The Dead End: The Road to Afghanistan*, ed. Svetlana Savranskaya and Malcolm Byrne (Washington, DC: National Security Archive, 2012), http://www.gwu.edu/~nsarchiv/NSAEBB/NSAEBB396/Full%20Text%20Virus%20A.pdf.

43. Braithwaite, *Afgantsy*, 89–94; Peter Tomsen, *The Wars of Afghanistan: Messianic Terrorism, Tribal Conflicts, and the Failures of Great Powers* (New York: Public Affairs, 2011), 171–78. Also see Aleksander A. Liakhovskii, *Tragediia i doblest' Afgana* [The Tragedy and Valor of the Afghan] (Moscow: GPI Iskona, 1995), 144–51; Khristoforov, *Afganistan*, 37–38; Bradsher, *Afghanistan and the Soviet Union*, 169–88.

44. "Remarks at a White House Briefing for Members of Congress," January 8, 1980 (first quote); *Meet the Press*, January 20, 1980 (second quote), *Public Papers of the Presidents of the United States, 1980–1981* (Washington, DC: Government Printing Office, 1981), 1:40, 111. For an overview of the U.S. response, see Bradsher, *Afghanistan and the Soviet Union*, 189–204.

45. "Budget Message," *Public Papers of the Presidents, 1980–81*, 1:230; Bradsher, *Afghanistan and the Soviet Union*, 190. For the Olympic boycott, see Nicholas E. Sarantakes, *Dropping the Torch: Jimmy Carter, the Olympic Boycott, and the Cold War* (New York: Cambridge University Press, 2011); Stephanie W. McConnell, "Jimmy Carter, Afghanistan, and the Olympic Boycott: The Last Crisis of the Cold War?" (PhD diss., Bowling Green State University, 2001).

46. Brzezinski has given slightly different variations to this story in interviews over the years, particularly in relation to covert U.S. aid that began in July 1979. For a parsing of his statements, see John B. White Jr., "The Strategic Mind of Zbigniew Brzezinski: How a Native Pole Used Afghanistan to Protect His Homeland" (master's thesis, Louisiana State University, 2012), 82–90, 97, http://etd.lsu.edu/docs/available/etd-04252012-175722/unrestricted/WHITE_THESIS.pdf.

47. Coll, *Ghost Wars*, 89–106. Operation Cyclone was the code name of the CIA program to arm, train, and finance the Afghan mujahideen. See also Thomas T. Hammond, *Red Flag over Afghanistan: The Communist Coup, the Soviet Invasion, and the Consequences* (Boulder, CO: Westview Press, 1984), 120–21.

48. Bradsher, *Afghanistan and the Soviet Union*, 227–37; Kakar, *Afghanistan*, 66–69; Liakhovskii, *Tragediia i doblest' Afgana*, 151–55.

49. *Military Balance, 1977–78*, 55–56; *Military Balance, 1979–80*, 62–63.

50. Braithwaite, *Afgantsy*, 136–39; Liakhovskii, *Tragediia i doblest' Afgana*, 178–80.

51. Lester W. Grau, trans. and ed., *The Bear Went over the Mountain: Soviet Combat Tactics in Afghanistan* (Washington, DC: National Defense University Press, 1996), offers Soviet views on tactics and operations in Afghanistan.

52. Liakhovskii, *Tragediia i doblest' Afgana*, 450; Khristoforov, *Afganistan*, 41–42; Braithwaite, *Afgantsy*, 140. This was the first of four major phases of the Soviet war in Afghanistan: phase one (December 1979–February 1980); phase two (March 1980–April 1985); phase three (April 1985–January 1987); and phase four (January 1987–February 1989). See Russian General Staff, *The Soviet-Afghan War: How a Superpower Fought and Lost*, trans. and ed. Lester W. Grau and Michael A. Gress (Lawrence: University Press of Kansas, 2002), 12–14, for descriptions of each phase.

53. Scott R. McMichael, "The Soviet Army, Counterinsurgency, and the Afghan War," *Parameters* 19 (December 1989): 21–35, http://strategicstudiesinstitute.army.mil/pubs/parameters/Articles/1989/1989%20mcmichael.pdf. As an example, Liakhovskii described his variable relationship and intermittent conflict with Ahmad Shah Massoud. Liakhovskii, *Tragediia i doblest' Afgana*, 494–525.

54. "Chemical Warfare in Afghanistan," Department of State report for Congress, March 22, 1982, *American Foreign Policy: Current Documents, 1982* (Washington, DC: Department of State, 1985), 909–12 (hereafter *AFP Current Docs*); "An Update on Chemical Warfare in Afghanistan," Department of State report for United Nations, November 1982, ibid., 919–20.

55. Russian General Staff, *Soviet-Afghan War*, 48–52.

56. The number increased to 750,000 by May 1980. Afghanistan Task Force, "Afghanistan," 4, 6. According to Kathleen Newland and Erin Patrick, more than six million Afghans became refugees during the 1980s. Newland and Patrick, "A Nation Displaced: The World's Largest Refugee Population," *WorldView* 14 (Fall 2001): 51–53, http://www.migrationpolicy.org/pubs/displaced.php.

57. Ronald W. Reagan, "Appeal to Soviet President Brezhnev for Peace in Afghanistan," March 20, 1982, *AFP Current Docs*, 907.

58. George H. W. Bush, speech, May 17, 1984, Peshawar, Pakistan, *AFP Current Docs, 1984*, 614.

59. Ibid., 614–15; Howard B. Schaffer, "Working Toward a Political Settlement while Continuing Our Support for the Resistance," statement before subcommittee on Asian and Pacific Affairs, House Committee on Foreign Affairs, June 14, 1989, *AFP Current Docs, 1989*, 466–67.

60. Kalinovsky, *Long Goodbye*, 16–44.

61. Ibid., 93–121.

62. Ibid., 113–14.

63. Ronald W. Reagan, statement by the president, June 16, 1986, *AFP Current Docs, 1986*, 472.

64. George Crile, *Charlie Wilson's War: The Extraordinary Story of the Largest Covert Operation in History* (New York: Atlantic Monthly Press, 2003).

65. Braithwaite, *Afgantsy*, 205.

66. Kalinovsky, *Long Goodbye*, 43. Edward B. Westermann, "The Limits of Soviet Airpower: The Failure of Military Coercion in Afghanistan, 1979–1989," *Journal of Conflict Studies* 19 (Fall 1989): 39–71, underlined the psychological importance of the Stinger missile since "accuracy and effectiveness of subsequent air operations suffered even more."

67. This was a complex, heavily debated, and extended process for Soviet leaders. See Kalinovsky, *Long Goodbye*, 147–77; Igor Tsybul'skii, *Boris Gromov* (Moscow: Molodaia gvardiia, 2008), 218–27.

68. Quoted in Baumann, *Russian-Soviet Unconventional Wars*, 148.

69. Lester W. Grau, "Breaking Contact Without Leaving Chaos: The Soviet Withdrawal from Afghanistan," *Journal of Slavic Military Studies* 20 (April 2007): 235–61.

70. Quoted in Gretchen Peters, *Seeds of Terror: How Drugs, Thugs, and Crime are Reshaping the Afghan Wars* (New York: Picador, 2010), 56.

71. John H. Kelly, "Policy Toward Afghanistan," March 7, 1990, *AFP Currents Docs, 1990,* 643.

72. "Joint Statement and Commentary issued by Secretary of State Baker and Soviet Foreign Minister Pankin," September 13, 1991, Moscow, USSR, *AFP Current Docs, 1991,* 650.

73. Kalinovsky, *Long Goodbye*, 206–8; Dorronsoro, *Revolution Unending*, 237–40.

74. Barfield, *Afghanistan*, 241.

75. Gen. Boris Gromov even wrote in a major Moscow newspaper in December 1999 that the Soviet invasion of Afghanistan was a huge political mistake. See Tsybul'skii, *Gromov*, 227.

76. Kalinovsky, *Long Goodbye*, 209; Dorronsoro, *Revolution Unending*, 235–37; Johnson, *Afghan Way of War*, 249–54.

Epilogue

1. Artemy M. Kalinovsky, *A Long Goodbye: The Soviet Withdrawal from Afghanistan* (Cambridge, MA: Harvard University Press, 2011), 107.

2. Thomas J. Barfield, *Afghanistan: A Cultural and Political History* (Princeton, NJ: Princeton University Press, 2010), 248.

3. Gilles Dorronsoro, *Revolution Unending: Afghanistan, 1979 to the Present* (New York: Columbia University Press, 2005), 237–38. Najibullah lived in the United Nations headquarters in Kabul until September 27, 1996, when Taliban soldiers took him to his torture and death.

4. The text of the accords is in Amera Saeed, "Afghanistan, Peshawar, and After," *Regional Studies* (Islamabad) 11, no. 2 (1993): 103–58.

5. Dorronsoro, *Revolution Unending*, 239.

6. Ibid., 240–50; Aleksandr A. Liakhovskii and Viacheslav Nekrasov, *Grazhdanin, Politik, Voin: Pamiati Akhmad Shakha Masuda* [Citizen, Politician, Warrior: In Memory of Ahmad Sheikh Massoud] (Moscow: n.p., 2007), 233–53; Peter Tomsen, *The Wars of Afghanistan: Messianic Terrorism, Tribal Conflicts, and the Failures of Great Powers* (New York: Public Affairs, 2011), 486–96.

7. Neamatollah Nojumi, "The Rise and Fall of the Taliban," in Robert D. Crews and Amin Tarzi, eds., *The Taliban and the Crisis of Afghanistan* (Cambridge, MA: Harvard University Press, 2008), 91.

8. Martin K. Ewans, *Afghanistan: A Short History of Its People and Politics* (New York: Perennial, 2002), 255.

9. Gretchen Peters, *Seeds of Terror: How Drugs, Thugs, and Crime are Reshaping the Afghan Wars* (New York: Picador, 2010), 74–75. See also Vanda Felbab-Brown, *Shooting Up: Counterinsurgency and the War on Drugs* (Washington, DC: Brookings Institution Press, 2010), ch. 5.

10. Nojumi, "Rise and Fall of the Taliban," 101; Dorronsoro, *Revolution Unending*, 246; Robert Johnson, *The Afghan Way of War: How and Why They Fight* (New York: Oxford University Press, 2011), 254–56.

11. Larry P. Goodson, *Afghanistan's Endless War: State Failure, Regional Politics, and the Rise of the Taliban* (Seattle: University of Washington Press, 2001), 108; Ahmed Rashid, *Taliban: Militant Islam, Oil, and Fundamentalism in Central Asia* (New Haven, CT: Yale University Press, 2000), 18–19, 84.

12. Olivier Roy, "Has Islamism a Future in Afghanistan?" in William Maley, ed., *Fundamentalism Reborn? Afghanistan and the Taliban* (New York: New York University Press, 1998), 211.

13. Kalinovsky, *Long Goodbye*, 211.

14. Brian Glyn Williams, *The Last Warlord: The Life and Legend of Dostum, the Afghan Warrior who led U.S. Special Forces to Topple the Taliban Regime* (Chicago, IL: Chicago Review Press, 2013), 161–207.

15. His battles with Soviet special forces took place in the spring of 1987. Ali H. Soufan with Daniel Freedman, *The Black Banners: The Inside Story of 9/11 and the War Against al-Qaeda* (New York: Norton, 2011), 63; Peter L. Bergen, *The Longest War: The Enduring Conflict between America and al-Qaeda* (New York: Free Press, 2011), 16.

16. Bergen, *Longest War*, 15.

17. For an overview of bin Laden's relationship with the Taliban, see Soufan, *Black Banners*, 52, 56–72; Bergen, *Longest War*, 11–35; Bruce O. Riedel, *The Search for Al Qaeda: Its Leadership, Ideology, and Future* (Washington, DC: Brookings Institution Press, 2008), 37–60; Lawrence Wright, *The Looming Tower: Al-Qaeda and the Road to 9/11* (New York: Knopf, 2006); Anonymous [Michael Scheuer], *Through Our Enemies' Eyes: Osama bin Laden, Radical Islam, and the Future of America* (Washington, DC: Brassey's, 2002), 151–93; *The 9/11 Commission Report: Final Report of the National Commission on Terrorist Attacks Upon the United* States (Washington, DC: U.S. Government Printing Office, 2004), 63–70; Priscilla D. Jones, *The First 109 Minutes: 9/11 and the U.S. Air Force* (Washington, DC: U.S. Air Force History and Museums Program, 2011), 46–51.

18. Rashid, *Taliban*, 133.

19. In April 1998, U.S. Ambassador to the United Nations William B. Richardson visited Afghanistan and requested that the Taliban expel bin Laden. He was the highest-ranking U.S. official to visit Afghanistan in decades. *9/11 Commission Report*, 111.

20. *9/11 Commission Report*, 65; Rashid, *Taliban*, 133.

21. John F. Burns, "Threats and Responses: Assassination; Afghans, Too, Mark a Day of Disaster: A Hero Was Lost," *New York Times*, September 9, 2002, http://www.nytimes.com/2002/09/09/world/threats-responses-assassination-afghans-too-mark-day-disaster-hero-was-lost.html.

22. Kalinovsky, *Long Goodbye*, 224–25.

23. Winston S. Churchill, *The Story of the Malakand Field Force* (1898; reprint, Mineola, NY: Dover Publications, 2010), 6.

MICHAEL R. ROULAND is a historian with the Naval History and Heritage Command, Washington, D.C. Before accepting this position in 2013, he worked for the U.S. Air Force Historical Studies Office in Washington, where he wrote this manuscript. He holds a doctorate in history from Georgetown University.

www.ingramcontent.com/pod-product-compliance
Lightning Source LLC
Chambersburg PA
CBHW080306290526
45790CB00005B/1946

* 9 781508 577218 *